.

THE
IRON
ACADEMY

FORGING YOUNG MEN WHO FIGHT FOR THE KING

ALAN HAHN, ED. D.

IRON FORGE PUBLISHING

Hardcover ISBN: 979-8-9987057-0-0
eBook ISBN: 979-8-9987057-2-4

Printed in the United States of America

This book was published with assistance of Goodwill Media Services Corp, **www.goodwillmediaservices.com.**

 Goodwill Media Services Corp.

DEDICATION

To my wife, Ann—my apple of gold in a setting of silver. Thank you for your boundless patience, steadfast love, and unwavering support throughout this journey. Your life would have been so much easier had I attended Iron Academy!

To the many godly people—Mike Brown, Dan Doster, Richard Mills, Lynn Greear, Bruce Mack, Bonnie Vacher, and others—who have invested their time and talent into sharpening me—your influence continues to echo in all I do. It had not occurred to me in the beginning of Iron Academy that I would require the most sharpening.

To the handful of men who showed me that the persistent, diligent pursuit of working hard for God's Kingdom pays extraordinary dividends—and that it is the proper way to order my life—thank you. Dave Rendall, Steve Maye, and Danny Lotz, your lives have marked mine. And to Dallas Willard— thank you for showing how to cut through life's noise and devote yourself wholly to what honors God—learning deeply, growing steadily, and serving faithfully. Your quiet focus still speaks volumes.

To Scott Michael—thank you for jumping in to be the first board president and helping launch a school unlike any other with conviction and clarity of vision.

To Rich Anderson—thank you for locking arms in the foxhole with me, serving as Principal (an often thankless job), offering wise counsel and thou-

sands of memorable metaphors, and remaining steadfast through all these years.

To the Iron Parents—thank you for the sacred trust of allowing me to play a meaningful role in your sons' lives. It is a blessing and responsibility I never take lightly.

To the Iron Staff—your daily commitment to revealing, as best we can, God's perfect design for young men is an act of worship. Your diverse talents and shared conviction make this mission real. Iron Academy is just a good idea without you.

To the Iron Board—thank you for modeling how to wield both rod and staff with wisdom, strength, and grace in a way that honors the Lord.

To the Iron Stakeholders—your belief and investment make this one-of-a-kind school a reality, year after year. Thank you for standing with us and giving so joyfully and generously.

And to the Iron Students—you are the reason this work matters. Thank you for choosing the harder path: the path of accountability, brotherly love, true community, and the sharpening that only comes from iron on iron.

May this work continue to sharpen generations to come—and build the Christ-centered brotherhood that is Iron Academy.

TABLE *of* CONTENTS

INTRODUCTION
Rediscovering Biblical Manhood

Manhood is in crisis. The virtues that once defined strong, honorable men—courage, integrity, wisdom, and faith—are vanishing in a culture that distorts masculinity and diminishes responsibility. A generation of young men drifts without purpose; women, children, entire families, churches, and communities suffer the consequences. But there is a way forward. Iron Academy is answering the call: raising up men of strength, conviction, and godly leadership. This is not the time for retreat. It is time to rebuild. Will we step up and restore the biblical foundation of manhood, or will we surrender to a culture that erases it?

"Else wherefore born?" *(Gareth, Idylls of the King)*

Whether or not King Arthur and his Knights of the Round Table truly existed, their stories continue to call young men to lives of honor, courage, and faith. These legends, grounded in chivalry, offer a timeless vision of what it means to live virtuously. Tales of chivalry emphasized living a life where worth was measured not by titles or wealth, but by purity, truth, and righteousness. Among these legends, the story of Gareth stands out as a powerful reminder of the moral urgency to "live pure, speak true, right wrong, and follow the King."

Gareth, the youngest son of Lot and Bellicent and nephew of King Arthur, was in his late teens—about the age of a high school senior.

Though born into nobility, Gareth longed for more than a life of comfort: he yearned for the honor and adventure of serving at the Knights of the Round Table. His mother, Bellicent, sought to keep him safe at home, surrounded by luxury. When Gareth pleaded to pursue his calling as a man of God, Bellicent urged him to remain a boy, playing in the woods and hunting deer.

But Gareth saw this as an attempt to extend his childhood, which he viewed as a form of slavery. He passionately declared, "Man am I grown, a man's work must I do. Follow the deer? Live pure, speak true, right wrong, and follow the King. Else, wherefore born?" In modern terms: "You want me to play in the woods instead of becoming a man? No! Why was I born if not to live with purity, speak truth, right wrongs, and follow the King?"

Gareth knew he was called to a higher purpose, one rooted in moral integrity, justice, and biblical virtues. His loyalty to King Arthur reflected his dedication to these principles and his desire to be a shepherd of the Kingdom. Though a fictional character, Gareth was crafted to inspire men—both young and old—to return to God-honoring conviction. Alfred, Lord Tennyson wrote *Idylls of the King* as part of his effort to revive Christian values in an England facing cultural and moral decline. Through Gareth's story, Tennyson recruited men ready to fight for the Kingdom of God, embodying virtues like purity, honesty, and justice. Gareth's desire to join the Knights of the Round Table was more than a pursuit of adventure—it was a commitment to protect the innocent and right wrongs. His loyalty to King Arthur, who symbolized Christ-like leadership, serves as a reminder to raise men who will stand firm in their faith and fight for Kingdom values with courage and conviction. The call is clear: **We must build generations of young men ready to follow the King and engage in the spiritual battle for the soul of our society.**

Tennyson's gift for writing powerful, evocative poetry was surpassed only by his specific call from the Holy Spirit to fight for the Kingdom of God through his art: a call to reclaim biblical virtue and build men. While gifts and callings hold great potential, they mean little without obedience. Appointed Poet Laureate by Queen Victoria, he used his literary talents to guide England back to God during a time of moral decline and societal change. Through works like *Idylls of the King,* Tennyson emphasized honor, justice, and faith in an era marked by debauchery, exploitation, and passivity. His poetry clearly urged a return to biblical principles. Critiquing the materialism of industrial society, Tennyson called for moral integrity and spiritual reflection, using his tenure to fulfill his divine mission of leading his generation back to Jesus. *Idylls of the King* rightly suggests that all Jesus-following people have a divine mission.

THE DECLINE OF MODERN MASCULINITY

Contrast Gareth's unwavering moral conviction, urgency, willingness to fight for virtue, and his exasperation—"Else, wherefore born?"—with modern American manhood. We no longer seem to embrace a male culture driven by an intense fighting spirit, resilience, and commitment to virtue. The Spirit of '76, the courage at the Alamo, and the determination of the Rough Riders are on the verge of cultural irrelevance. The valor of the Doughboys, the resolve of the Marines at Iwo Jima, and the bravery on D-Day once defined the American character. Today, however, male culture is—different.

Since the 1960s, traditional masculinity—courage, resilience, standing up for what is right, and even defending women—has come under scrutiny. While the push for gender equality brought positive change, it also contributed to a cultural shift that often devalues the distinct strengths and responsibilities of men. This shift has weakened the very qualities that once drove American men to embrace a fierce commitment to virtue, honor, chivalry, responsibility, and the defense of freedom. The roaring fighting spirit that once propelled generations to take bold stands for their families, communities, and nation is fading into a whimper.

The fighting spirit of the American male once also included defending the Christian faith and biblical virtue. The Puritans built early colonies on God-fearing leadership. The Founding Fathers established virtue and morality as cornerstones of the new republic. American men often served as spiritual shepherds—whether on the frontier, in the Victorian home, fighting to end slavery, or practicing civil disobedience during the Civil Rights Movement—they answered the call to lead with a steadfast commitment to God-honoring values.

---

1. *What kind of man do you want your son or grandson to be?*

2. *How is the current culture influencing boys' understanding of masculinity differently than when you were their age?*

3. *If your son/grandson asked you, "Else wherefore born?"—what answer would you give him?*

4. *What intentional steps do we take as a culture to ensure our sons/grandsons do not merely drift into adulthood, but are forged into God-honoring men?*

THE CONSEQUENCES OF ERODED MANHOOD

Since the 1960s, Americans have witnessed a troubling decline in traditional male roles, leading to profound consequences for families and society as a whole. Over the past fifty years, the normalization and even celebration of men fathering children outside marriage has devalued the marriage union and harmed women and children. It weakens life-giving family structures and erodes the former stability of marriage. Human trafficking and sexual slavery at the hands of predatory men are on the rise, causing severe trauma and trapping victims in cycles of abuse and exploitation. The normalization of abortion—including barbaric late-term procedures—devalues life and sadly reflects a culture where men neglect their roles as providers, justifying their basest desires.

Nominal Christian men, with shallow faith, are more prone to divorce and domestic abuse; this undermines the foundations necessary for strong marriages. Cultural expectations for men are diminishing, as seen in declining education, extended adolescence, reduced workforce participation, and the normalization of non-traditional family roles. Young men are increasingly disengaged from the church, weakening their spiritual leadership in families and contributing to the decline of male involvement in evangelical congregations.

Joshua 1:9 (ESV): "Have I not commanded you? Be strong and courageous. Do not be frightened, and do not be dismayed, for the LORD your God is with you wherever you go."

A SPIRITUAL CRISIS

Many of society's ills—from crime to poverty, from broken homes to the exploitation of the vulnerable, to rising abortion rates and the increasing acceptability of late-term abortion—are directly related to unbiblical manhood. Young men are increasingly abandoning their spiritual responsibilities, leaving a void where strong, God-honoring men should stand. We must urgently reclaim our role in raising Christian boys into men who embody the virtues of faith, responsibility, and protection. The time to act is now: to restore the values that once fortified our families and communities and to build a future where men rise to their God-given call to lead, protect, and uphold the sanctity of life, marriage, and family.

THE FIGHT FOR BIBLICAL MANHOOD

So, what are we to fight? For decades, our answer has been to fight *against* men. That has not worked. Since the 1960s, the U.S. has seen a decline in areas that once made it a global beacon of hope and prosperity for families, especially in the treatment of women and children. From rising maternal mortality rates and child poverty to diminishing safety for women, our nation is no longer the leader in quality of life it once was. This decline demands a return to the values and commitments that once ensured a brighter future for every generation.

While ungodly manhood must always be confronted, the relentless attack on men over the last five decades has resulted in an emasculated, confused, and unfocused masculinity in America, one that hurts everyone. When biblical manhood is absent, women and children suffer. But when men rise to pursue biblical manhood—a manhood that reflects biblical virtues and the qualities of a loving shepherd—everyone wins. The fight must be *for men*. Specifically, we must fight with renewed intentionality to raise Christian boys into godly men!

> 5. *How do women and children suffer when we fail to build God-honoring men?*
>
> 6. *"Everyone wins?" Would everyone really win if men emulated Jesus to the best of their ability?*
>
> 7. *"The fight must be for men?" What evidence do we have that our fight against men has failed?*

A Call to Holiness

J.C. Ryle, an Anglican preacher in the 1870s, found himself disgusted with the passivity of men within the Church of England. In response, he wrote an extraordinarily powerful treatise on actively walking the path of righteousness and pursuing the holiness that God desires for us and from us. In *Holiness*, he shares a thought that has captivated me and shaped my daily life: "He who would understand the nature of true holiness must know that the Christian is a 'man of war.' If we would be holy, we must fight!" (*Holiness*, 1877)

In other words, true holiness requires recognizing that it involves a constant spiritual battle. Holiness demands actively fighting against sin and evil. It requires aggressive, intentional action. *We must fight!* With overwhelming evidence against what has been done *to* and *for* men in the United States since the 1960s, there has never been a time of greater urgency to fight than right now. *We must fight!* Not against flesh and blood, but against sin, passivity, complacency, and the destructive notion of "good enough." *We must fight for* our sons and grandsons, striving to reveal God's inerrant design for them as warriors for His Kingdom on Earth.

Holiness as a culture requires fighting for better men. If we are to be a God-honoring people, we must fight for our sons and grandsons. We must fight for them to become good shepherds, diligent workers and keepers of the Kingdom, loving and faithful husbands, committed and fully engaged fathers, and strong and courageous men who love well. This will never happen by accident.

8. *In your own words, what was J.C. Ryle saying when he wrote, "If we would be holy, we must fight?"*

9. *How might the boys and men today be like the boys and men of Ryle's England?*

10. *What does passivity look like in men within the Church today? In families? Be specific.*

MY CALL TO THE FIGHT!

Every generation brings opportunity for those who profess submission to Jesus Christ to fight for the Kingdom of Heaven. In many ways, our age is no different from those before it; yet how can we not feel a grave sense of urgency today to fight with all our being for the cause of Christ? As Jesus declared, "Behold, the Kingdom of God is in your midst!"

Throughout history, God has called both the prominent and the ordinary to lead His people back to Him during times of spiritual and moral decline. Ordinary individuals like Gideon, Esther, Jesus' fishermen disciples, Mary (Jesus' mother), and Priscilla were empowered by God to accomplish extraordinary tasks. Likewise, figures like St. Augustine, Martin Luther, John Wesley, Richard Allen, Harriet Tubman, Andrew Murray, Charles Octavius Boothe, Corrie ten Boom, Billy Graham, Elisabeth Elliot, Byang Kato, and Chuck Colson played pivotal roles in reviving faith and biblical truth in their eras. This pattern continues today, reminding us that God's call is not limited by human qualifications but is a normal and expected part of the Christian life, meant for every believer.

If the call is a normal occurrence—something to be expected as a follower of Christ—it is also normal to reject the call. We see this all the time in our daily lives. After all, God's calling can feel quite overwhelming. Who are we to be tapped on the shoulder by the Creator of the universe to do something big? Even Moses shrank from God's calling at the burning bush, asking, "Who am I that I should go to Pharaoh and that I should bring the sons of Israel out of Egypt?"

God was preparing me for my "Moses moment" soon after we returned from living in Venezuela. After four years of marriage, during which I was woefully unprepared to be the man Ann needed—both as a husband or as a father—I finally submitted to Jesus' lordship over my life. I left my work teaching Spanish-speaking inmates, serving as the national lead Spanish-language instructor for staff, and working as a hostage negotiator for the Federal Bureau of Prisons to teach 11th and 12th graders in a Christian high school.

In my second year there, it became clear that, despite the school's beauty and size, it was mostly graduating boys—not young men who knew who they were in Christ and what it meant to be godly men. I realized this was not just a problem at one school but across the country, where high schools and colleges were producing boys instead of God-honoring men. Worse, women were marrying boys, hoping they would mature into godly men. To my shame, that is exactly what my Ann had to do. Even as a very immature Christian, I could see the need for an uber-intentional environment that would help parents build boys into godly men.

Eden's Iron Story:

Before attending Iron Academy, I was at a private Christian school where I felt constant pressure to be perfect. Mistakes led to punishment, and I never felt truly accepted for who I was. The environment left me feeling lost and unsure of my path.

Stepping into Iron Academy was like a breath of fresh air after the suffocating pressure of my previous school. From my very first day in the middle of the school year, I was welcomed with acceptance and understanding. I learned very quickly that Iron Academy teachers didn't talk about "punishment" and they didn't get angry. When people messed up, they received burpees—and sometimes lots of them—but it was always for the right reasons. Things weren't about behavior control. They didn't expect perfection. They definitely have standards, but they let you be guys. That made a big difference. We could be who we really were. We didn't have to fake anything. In fact, that's one of the biggest differences: fakes didn't fit in at Iron.

They taught me that accountability isn't about being flawless; it's about starting from where you are and growing from there. The Honor Code—"I will always conduct myself as a gentleman, live pure, speak true, right wrong, and follow the King"—encouraged me to strive for excellence while accepting my imperfections.

The transition to Iron Academy wasn't easy, and I had my doubts. But the unwavering support from teachers and fellow students made all the difference. I saw that at Iron Academy, younger kids looked up to the older kids, and the older kids treated the younger kids really well. It seemed so strange to me in a school, but people loved each other. That took some getting used to!

I was given the opportunity to step into leadership roles: I became a tribe leader, a captain of the basketball team, and even the elected school leader. Iron Academy didn't just help me see my potential; it pushed me to be the best version of myself, inspiring personal growth and leadership. Iron gave me confidence.

Looking back, I realize that without Iron Academy, I might have remained lost, lacking direction and confidence. Iron Academy's focus on building strong, educated, and faith-driven young men provided the foundation I needed. This foundation led me to graduate from college with Cum Laude honors. Iron Academy isn't just a school; it's a guiding light that helps boys become men of integrity, discipline, and faith, shaping their futures with confidence and direction. And the relationship does not end with graduation. My Iron story isn't over. Iron is part of me. Forever.

(Eden Ondachi, 2020 Iron Graduate)

MY MOSES MOMENT

My "Moses moment" came when God began placing people in my life who kept saying, "You should start a boys' school." Family, friends, colleagues, even students echoed the same message. Seeking wisdom, I turned to my church for counsel, wanting to be sure this wasn't just my ego talking. But the calling was unmistakable. Yet, like Moses, I was terrified. "Who am I, Lord, to start a boys' school? I'm just a teacher. I don't have the resources. There are better men than me for this."

Still, being at that time the semi-obedient man I was, I began making plans—but only for the possibility of opening a school fifteen years in the future. Why fifteen years? Because it was far enough away to feel unreal. It was a nebulous goal—one I could conveniently ignore. I started my doctoral work in education so that I could be qualified to do what God was asking of me. I took on more leadership roles at the school where I worked, hoping to become more competent for this undeniable calling on my life. I stepped into greater responsibilities at church. I was doing the things I thought the world would expect from someone crazy enough to think he should start a school.

Fifteen years leaves plenty of time to prepare for obedience. It even allowed me to convince myself I was being obedient.

Years later—yes, years later—Ann and I were in a small group discussion of Numbers chapter 13. In this chapter, God instructed Moses to send twelve men, one from each tribe of Israel, to explore the land of Canaan, the promised land, described as "flowing with milk and honey." For forty days, the spies explored the land, confirming its extraordinary abundance but also encountering powerful inhabitants and heavily fortified cities—including the feared Anakim, the giants.

Despite witnessing countless miracles during their journey, the parting of the Red Sea, manna from heaven, water from a rock, the Israelites allowed fear to overshadow their faith. While Caleb and Joshua urged the people to trust in God and take possession of the land, the other ten spies gave a fearful report, leading the Israelites to doubt God's promise. Instead of stepping forward in faith, they longed to return to Egypt, unwilling to face what they perceived as insurmountable challenges.

Their exact words were, "We saw the Nephilim (the giants), and we seemed to ourselves like grasshoppers, and so we seemed to them." Despite the miracles and God's providence, ten of Israel's chosen leaders—men of strength, men of influence—shrank from God's purpose for their lives and saw themselves as nothing more than grasshoppers. And because they saw themselves as small and insignificant, they became exactly that.

> **Numbers 13:32–33 (ESV): "So they brought to the people of Israel a bad report of the land that they had spied out, saying, 'The land, through which we have gone to spy it out, is a land that devours—inhabitants, and all the people that we saw in it are of great height. And there we saw the Nephilim (the sons of Anak, who come from the Nephilim), and we seemed to ourselves like grasshoppers, and so we seemed to them.'"**

"Those stupid Israelites!"

Every time I had read this account—or any number of others in the Old Testament—I couldn't help but feel frustrated with the Israelites. They followed a ridiculously predictable pattern from which they never seemed to learn the obvious lesson: obey God. When they faithfully followed Him, they prospered, enjoying His blessings and protection. But over time, they would drift away, falling into idolatry and moral decay, leading to suffering and oppression. In their distress, they would cry out to God, repent, and return to Him—only to be restored and once again experience His provision. This cycle repeated itself over and over, underscoring God's unwavering faithfulness and mercy—yet also their repeated failure to learn from past mistakes.

Those stupid Israelites, indeed! How could the ten tribal leaders not stand with Joshua and Caleb, ready to claim God's promises and follow His lead? As God says in Isaiah 65:2, "I spread out my hands all the day to rebellious people, who walk in a way that is not good, following their own devices." There it was—the truth, plain as day. They were disobedient and rebellious people. Those stupid Israelites.

It was obvious to the whole small group. But then Kevin, a friend in the group, suddenly declared, "That's the grasshopper complex!" And with those words, my life was forever changed.

I immediately recognized the Numbers 13 story—those ridiculous Israelites—was just as much about me, Alan Hahn. Like the Israelites, God had given abundant evidence of His providence and power. Like the Israelites, He had given me a mission. Like the Israelites, I considered the mission too big. I justified my semi-obedience, convincing myself that preparing over the next nebulous fifteen years was enough. There were giants standing in my way, and instead of trusting God, I had chosen to see myself as a grasshopper... And so, I became a grasshopper.

That realization changed everything. I decided to stop doubting and follow the examples of Joshua and Caleb. The very next day, I approached Scott Michael about becoming the board president for the school. Shortly after, Ann came up with the perfect name: Iron Academy—inspired by Proverbs 27:17, "As iron sharpens iron, so one man sharpens another." Rich Anderson was all in too. Risking a great deal, he would leave the relative ease and predictability of a safe and established Christian school to launch Iron Academy with me. We were like Frodo Baggins and Samwise Gamgee leaving the Shire in *Lord of the Rings*—stepping into the unknown, driven by a mission greater than ourselves. The comforts of home were behind us, and ahead lay uncertainty, challenges, and giants (and worse!) to face. But just as the hobbits had their fellowship, God was assembling ours. With a clear calling and the beginning of a team in place, I knew it was time to cross into the Promised Land, like stepping into Mordor, where the real battle awaited. It was time to fight the giants, not with swords, but with faith, conviction, and the certainty that the mission was worth every hardship.

11. *Is there anything resembling the "grasshopper complex" in your life?*

12. *What kind of team would it take to launch a school? What would the various roles be on that team?*

IRON ACADEMY: BUILDING MEN FOR GOD'S KINGDOM

This book is about that fight. Specifically, it is about Iron Academy's historically unique calling and gifting to build men. Throughout history, few intentional communities have been dedicated to guiding boys in understanding and living out God's perfect design for them as men. Early monastic communities, chivalric orders, Puritan societies, the Clapham Sect, and the YMCA all sought to instill virtues like discipline, courage, and moral integrity, grounded in biblical principles.

Unlike anything else in the last two thousand years, Iron Academy emulates the best aspects of these movements while keeping unwavering focus on biblical outcomes—building men who will be shepherds within their families, communities, and churches. We incorporate the spiritual discipline of monastic communities, the courage and moral integrity of the chivalric orders, the joy and camaraderie of David and Jonathan, and the leadership training of the Puritans, all while avoiding the pitfalls of legalism, asceticism, overemphasis on external accomplishments, and political vicissitudes.

At Iron Academy, our holistic approach ensures that young men are not only equipped with biblical virtues and the best lessons from history but are also deeply rooted in their identity as men of God, fully prepared to lead and serve with wisdom, compassion, and strength in every area of life.

> 13. *Why do you think it is that we have so few historical examples of intentional communities primarily dedicated to building God-honoring men?*

THE FIGHT BEGINS NOW

The fight, then, is for men. The fight is for this Iron model to flourish, expand into new areas, and serve as a blueprint for parents and grandparents everywhere, transforming the way we approach our calling to build boys into men. I pray you will join this fight.

While the future health or decline of our country undoubtedly depends on the kind of men we raise, an even greater reality remains: God has called us to this mission. Regardless of the cultural shifts in our nation, we are commanded to build up godly men within our Jesus-following communities. We may have limited influence over government schooling, but it is morally imperative that we embrace our calling to fight for our boys, to equip them to become God-honoring, life-giving shepherds.

The following chapters will lay out how we must fight to reclaim God-honoring manhood, build boys into men, and reaffirm your divine mission in this fight. These chapters will provide a biblical blueprint for manhood that benefits everyone, clarify the Iron Principles that guide boys in their journey to become men, reacquaint you with the historical significance of rites of passage, expose the greatest failing within American youth culture, and challenge you to join the Fight Club!

If you're still reading, my guess is you, too, are often considered radical. But perhaps the more accurate word is biblical. If that is true, you are called to this fight. You are called to join us in the foxhole. Just as in Numbers 13, the giants stand against us, but God stands with us. We were created for this. Let our fight begin!

14. The notion of joining us in the foxhole is not a frivolous choice of words. Reflecting on the introduction, what is it about Iron Academy's calling that would compel people from all over the country to commit considerable financial resources to launch a community like Iron Academy? What would compel someone like Rich Anderson, a husband and a father of five, to take an enormous risk to help launch this kind of school?

THE BIBLICAL BLUEPRINT *for* MANHOOD *That* BENEFITS EVERYONE

Thanks, thanks to thee, my worthy friend, For the lesson thou hast taught! Thus at the flaming forge of life Our fortunes must be wrought; Thus on its sounding anvil shaped Each burning deed and thought.

(From "The Village Blacksmith" by Henry Wadsworth Longfellow)

CHAPTER 1

MEN AND METAL

Swords captivate men. They always have, and they always will. From the moment a three-year-old grabs the tube from the middle of the Christmas wrapping paper, the fascination begins, and it never really ends. Men are drawn to swords; there is something about them that speaks to the soul of a man. At some point, most men have dreamed of being a blacksmith—forging something strong, shaping metal with fire and force. I still like the idea of having a forge in the backyard, but nothing is ever quite as easy as it seems.

Mastering the craft of swordsmithing is a highly challenging and time-intensive pursuit, requiring a blend of technical skill, artistic precision, and functional knowledge of metallurgy. A swordsmith must learn to shape, heat-treat, and temper various types of steel to create blades that strike the perfect balance of strength, sharpness, and flexibility. This ancient craft demands not only technical expertise but also creativity and an understanding of time-honored techniques—from the folding steel of the Japanese katana to the pattern-welding of Viking swords. True mastery in swordsmithing takes decades of apprenticeship and practice; few of us have the patience for that.

Throughout history, master swordsmiths were revered for their rare and exceptional abilities, crafting weapons that were more than just tools of war—they were symbols of status, artistry, and power. In cultures such as medieval Europe, feudal Japan, and the Viking era, these craftsmen played a pivotal role in shaping military strength by forging superior blades that gave warriors a distinct advantage in battle. Swords like the Japanese katana and medieval European Ulfberht were prized for their craftsmanship, strength, and spiritual significance. Though industrialization nearly led to the extinction of traditional blacksmithing techniques, a resurgence of interest in the late 1900s has preserved this ancient craft. Today, artisans and enthusiasts continue to celebrate its rich history, working to rediscover and refine its secrets.

Now, we have men fully committed to the art of swordsmithing—masters who have reclaimed historic expertise. Yoshindo Yoshihara, a tenth-generation Japanese swordsmith, continues the ancient tradition of katana-making with unparalleled artistry, earning worldwide acclaim. Howard Clark, an American smith, merges traditional techniques with modern metallurgy, producing swords that are both beautiful and highly functional. David DelaGardelle brings a deep understanding of medieval and Viking sword designs, blending history and craftsmanship in each unique piece. These masters exemplify the revival of ancient swordsmithing, forging works that honor tradition while integrating modern innovation.

TWO SWORDS

Iron Academy has two swords, both crafted by David DelaGardelle of Cedarlore Forge. Though he is now one of the greatest swordsmiths alive, we have his very first sword. When I show it to young men, their eyes widen, and their faces brighten. They immediately recognize it as a sword; they want to hold it. They are drawn to it. Yet, while it is clearly a sword, it has flaws. Smithing a sword is incredibly difficult, and David's first attempt shows it. It is rustic, rough, and rigid. The blade is misshapen; the cross guard is an old railroad tie. The grip is too thin; it is uncomfortable to hold. The pommel is loosely riveted and serves no real purpose. It is unbalanced and not sharp. It has some rust and lacks beauty.

And yet you could fight with it. Every boy who sees it wants to hold it. Even an ugly sword is still a sword, and that makes it special. That sword represents modern biblical manhood. It is rare, and it stands out; we are drawn to it. It commands attention; it probably scares some people. But it isn't all it could have been. It's a bit awkward and uncomfortable; it's not sharp. It's a little rusty. You could still call upon it in an emergency, but you might question its effectiveness. When put to the test, it might just break.

David was not yet a master craftsman. He had learned a lot, but building a sword requires significant expertise. I've been told that forging a sword is the equivalent of earning a master's degree in an academic area; most people never reach that level of skill. Had David known more, had he possessed greater mastery, he would have crafted a better sword.

Frankly, that sword is Alan Hahn. All the ingredients were there from the beginning. God designed me—and every Jesus-follower—to serve His Kingdom in powerful ways. Within my DNA is His design for me to fight. But, like David's first sword, I did not receive the proper heating, the appropriate hammering, the correct tempering, the complete deburring, or the precise sharpening in my early years. Or perhaps, more accurately, I did not avail myself to the people who were trying to forge me. As a result, I am not what I could have been. I am not yet all God had in mind for me. Though I am a Jesus-follower today and He is unquestionably leading me along the path of righteousness, I rejected His design for many years. The world still has its ill effects folded into my being. But, slowly, surely, I am being transformed by the renewal of my mind to His plan.

But we have another of David's swords. It is beautiful. David has followers from all over the world who admire his craftsmanship, and many have expressed that the Iron Academy sword is among his finest work. The cross guard is strong, straight, and elegantly shaped. The blade is true and razor-sharp; I've cut myself on it twice! It is perfectly tempered and balanced. The fuller adds rigidity while reducing overall weight. The pommel is sized for ideal balance but also serves its original purpose: to deliver a non-fatal blow. The grip, wrapped in vegetable-tanned leather, is comfortable and secure. The scabbard, crafted from a single piece of cherry wood, is a work of art. This is a remarkable weapon, among the best in the world. Engraved on one side of the sword are the words, "Because biblical manhood is never an accident." Never. That sword represents what our young men should become. It is what they were meant to become.

1. *What parallels are there between modern biblical manhood and David DelaGardelle's first sword?*

2. *Unpack the sentiment that the Iron Academy sword—among the best swords made in the last 100 years—presents a picture of God's true design for biblical manhood?*

3. *How is it possible that the two swords—made by the same person—could be so different? How is that helpful for us to understand our role in raising boys into godly men?*

4. *How is forging a sword a metaphor for revealing God's design for young men?*

5. *In terms of embracing the call all of us have in building boys into God-honoring men, do you feel more like David when he shaped his first sword or when he forged the Iron Academy sword? Explain.*

With expertise and intentionality comes conformity to God's design. Bringing raw metal to the proper temperature makes it malleable. Precise hammering and shaping come from thousands of hours of skill-building. Tempering in an oil bath at the exact temperature and time produces shocking flexibility and the ability to absorb impact without breaking. The final product is deburred, sharpened, and polished—presentable to society and ready for the fight.

What's the difference between the two swords? The Iron Academy sword is the result of mastery of skill, attention to detail, and patience. David DelaGardelle was driven by passion and pride in his craft, balancing traditional techniques with creativity, all while maintaining extraordinarily high standards throughout the process. His dedication ensured that the

Iron Academy sword was not just functional but superbly crafted, both in performance and in beauty. The first sword is likely worthless to anyone else; the second sword—the Iron Academy sword—is worth several thousand dollars.

In today's world, we place little value on swords. Most available options are cheap, unbalanced, and unreliable—certainly not something you'd stake your life on. And yet, this parallels how we approach building boys into extraordinary, God-honoring men. We don't invest thousands of hours learning how to do it. We don't dedicate the necessary time, talent, and energy to cultivate biblical manhood. Instead, we settle for mediocre results where a man is considered "better" simply because he doesn't exhibit the most glaring failures of our culture.

"Good Enough" or God's Blueprint

As good Christians, we often settle for "good enough." We applaud men simply for avoiding the worst behaviors—abandonment, addiction, dishonesty—without calling them to strive for godliness. This lowered standard trickles down to middle and high school boys. We deem them acceptable simply because they aren't engaging in obvious misconduct: not using drugs, not tattooing their faces, not getting anyone pregnant, not obsessing over their gender identity. Whether we are referring to adult men or schoolboys, we fail to pursue the higher standard of biblical manhood. We neglect the call to cultivate deep character, faith, and spiritual growth. As radical Jesus-people, however, the standard for Bible-based manhood remains unchanged.

6.   *What does it mean to settle for "good enough?"*
     What are the costs of settling for "good enough"
     when building boys into young men?

7.   *Why is "good enough" such an alluring trap?*

Ezra 7:9b–10 (ESV): "The good hand of his God was on him for Ezra had set his heart to study the Law of the Lord, and to do it and to teach his statutes and rules in Israel."

Godly men are called to live out the Ezra 7:10 model of studying God's Word, practicing biblical wisdom throughout every domain of life, and teaching other people to live the life Jesus demonstrates. They must lead their families and communities in spiritual leadership, guiding others in discipleship and embracing the role of the shepherd. They must exhibit humility and teachability, recognizing their dependence on God and remaining open to correction. Living with integrity and uprightness provides trust and security to those they lead. Practicing self-control and discipline ensures their actions align with godly values. Standing firm in faith with courage and perseverance, even through trials, characterizes true manhood. Leading by serving others follows Christ's example of servanthood. Living in community allows them to embody love, compassion, and hospitality while shepherding, protecting, and nurturing God's people.

8.   *What are the three components of Ezra's model*
     and how are they directly applicable to our lives?
     Are there any areas in which you could/should
     grow that the Ezra principle does not apply?

This is the biblical standard. This is the call. And this is what we must pursue. The world doesn't need more men who are simply "good enough"; it needs men who, like David's second sword, have been carefully forged, properly tempered, and skillfully sharpened for God's purposes.

A Glance at the Biblical Qualities Intended for Men

QUALITY	EXPLANATION	BIBLE REFERENCES
Pursuing God	Men who find favor with the Lord commit themselves to study God's Word and practice living God's Word. Furthermore, they endeavor to share what they know with others, expanding the Kingdom of God.	Ezra 7:10
Spiritual Leadership	Godly men lead their families and communities in faith—guiding others in discipleship and reflecting the Lord's role as a shepherd who leads, protects, and restores.	Ephesians 5:23; 1 Timothy 3:2–5; Titus 1:9; Psalm 23:2–3
Humility and Teachability	They exhibit humility, recognizing their dependence on God, remaining open to correction and growth—trusting in His guidance and embracing a teachable spirit.	Philippians 2:3; 1 Peter 5:5; Psalm 23:2–3

Integrity and Uprightness	Godly men walk in integrity, remaining blameless in their conduct, and providing security and trust—much like the shepherd who leads with righteousness.	Proverbs 10:9; 1 Timothy 3:2; Titus 1:6–7; Psalm 23:3
Self-Control and Discipline	They exercise self-control and discipline, displaying the fruit of the Spirit and ensuring their actions align with godly values.	Galatians 5:22-23; 1 Timothy 3:2; Titus 1:8; Psalm 23:2
Courage and Perseverance	Godly men stand firm in faith, showing courage and perseverance through challenges—trusting in God's protection, much like the shepherd in the valley.	Joshua 1:9; 1 Corinthians 16:13; 1 Timothy 3:12; Psalm 23:4
Servanthood	They lead by serving others, laying down their lives for the well-being of those they guide, following Christ's example of servant leadership.	Mark 10:45; 1 Peter 5:2; Psalm 23:1
Love, Compassion, and Hospitality	Godly men show love, compassion, and hospitality, tending to others' needs and fostering nurturing relationships, creating a safe, loving environment.	1 Peter 3:7; 1 Timothy 3:2; Titus 1:8; Psalm 23:4–5

Failing to properly invest in boys yields terrible results—grieving God, harming women and children, and tearing apart our nation. Pick up any national or regional paper, and you will undoubtedly find countless examples of men falling short of godly manhood: sexual misconduct, abuse of power, family abandonment, infidelity, dishonesty, sexual depravity, and violence.

These behaviors violate biblical principles of purity, integrity, and responsibility, causing deep harm to those around them. Men who abuse power or betray their families contribute to the breakdown of trust and the erosion of moral leadership. These failures do more than damage personal lives—they weaken the very fabric of society. This crisis highlights the urgent need to raise boys into godly men who will lead with integrity, humility, and love.

It is our urgent responsibility to step in, teach, mentor, and disciple the next generation into the men God designed them to be—men who will uphold righteousness, protect their families, and serve their communities with a spirit of sacrifice and love. The time to act is now. There is a better way, and it begins with people radically committed to biblical principles.

9. *Challenge: For the next month, read the chapter of Proverbs that matches the day's date (e.g., on the 8th, read Proverbs 8). Each day, identify the qualities of God and the qualities He calls us to reflect. For example, Proverbs 8:13 urges us to reject pride and arrogance, while the chapter as a whole teaches that pursuing wisdom is pursuing God's very nature—His righteousness, justice, and truth. We do this by actively seeking wisdom, loving truth, rejecting evil, fearing the Lord, trusting His design, and daily submitting to His instruction. Write down your observations in your Bible. Wrestle with who God is and who He calls you to be—it will change you. If this daily practice strengthens you, keep going for a year... or for life.*

Virtue in Literature:

The instruction of English in schools may be considered overly subjective when compared to the harder sciences of Algebra or Chemistry. After all, we are instructed early in our academic careers to look for climaxes in a reading and then told later that a work may or may not have one at all.

Students even come to prefer a subject like Algebra precisely because there is not room for subjectivity. Two and two make four, the square of five is twenty-five, solve for "x." The world can be described in numbers, and sums can be proven or disproven.

What is not often reflected upon is that most of these "harder" sciences are based in abstractions; a student can know quite a bit about photosynthesis but will not ever see it. A young man can know that Stalin was raised in Georgia, but his existence remains as abstract as nuclear fusion to the high school student.

If, however, English class is grounded in virtue, then literature is as observable as evaporation. Everyone can experience bravery just as they experience steam—a young man can feel his courage tested as plainly as he can feel condensation on his skin. Through literature, he not only observes virtue, but also experiences it vicariously. He walks with characters through trials and triumphs, faces their moral dilemmas, and wrestles with fear and failure—all without suffering real-world consequences. These stories provide a proving ground where he learns, through the lives of others, how courage, wisdom, and integrity shape a man's destiny. Knowledge of Christian love and hope remains in the mind and soul far longer than the quadratic formula. Experience and love of virtue is, in fact, the only reason to study literature.

At Iron Academy, each of our books is selected for the heavenly, cardinal, and theological virtues it contains. We subscribe to the wisdom of Paul and believe that a man can know and say many intelligent things, but all is as a clanging cymbal or tinkling bell without love and its accompanying virtues.

(Patrick Billinghurst, English Teacher)

NEVER AN ACCIDENT

The crafting of a sword is a deliberate and painstaking process, and so too must be the formation of boys into men who reflect God's design. This does not happen by accident. It requires intentional investment, mentorship, and proven methods that cultivate biblical manhood. As radically Jesus-following people, we are called to more than mediocrity. We are called to actively pursue God's true design for boys, shaping them into the men they were created to be.

The time to act is now, and the method is clear. Proven frameworks rooted in Scripture, discipleship, and the science behind God's design for males offer the roadmap. Will we rise to the challenge and commit to this sacred work, or will we continue to settle for less than God's best for our sons, our families, our country, or His Kingdom?

The next chapter lays out a radical yet proven model for intentionally shaping boys into godly men. It is a method deeply rooted in Scripture, discipleship, and an understanding of God's design for males. This approach fosters the deep character and spiritual maturity that true biblical manhood requires—a manhood that blesses everyone it touches.

The Bible sets a high standard for manhood—one that demonstrates a love for God and a love for people. Micah 6:8 calls men to live justly, show mercy, and walk humbly with God, cultivating fairness, compassion, and humility that not only strengthen their faith but also nurture fair play and kindness in their relationships with others. 1 Corinthians 16:13–14 commands men to stand firm in faith, exhibit strength, courage, and love in their actions, modeling faithfulness and care that protects and uplifts women, children, and communities. Similarly, Ephesians 5:25–28 calls husbands to love their wives as Christ loves the Church, leading with self-sacrificial love and respect, creating a family environment where women and children flourish.

In 1 Timothy 3:1–7, the qualities of elders and overseers—self-control, respectability, and leadership—set a high standard for all men. These virtues cultivate integrity in family life, creating stable homes that strengthen society. Likewise, 1 Timothy 3:8–12 highlights the importance of integrity and responsibility in deacons, showing that men who manage their households well contribute to ethical, trustworthy communities where others are treated with dignity. Genesis 2:15 illustrates man's role as a steward, calling men to be diligent in their responsibilities, whether in work, family, or faith. A man's stewardship promotes care and support for all those under his influence.

In Proverbs 27:17, men are called to accountability and mutual growth, sharpening one another in their journey to become godlier men—a practice that positively impacts marriages, friendships, and society at large. Titus 1:6–9 emphasizes faithfulness and moral integrity, qualities that equip men to guide their families and communities with wisdom and righteousness, fostering environments of trust and ethical leadership. Finally, Titus 2:2 encourages older men to model self-control, dignity, love, and steadfast faith, providing younger men with examples of maturity—a discipleship that builds stronger, more disciplined families and communities.

When men embody these biblical virtues—integrity, love, responsibility, and humility—they become better husbands, fathers, and leaders, aligning with the values of courage, integrity, leadership, and service. These qualities not only strengthen their families but also positively impact society, fostering healthier, more supportive relationships where women, children, and others are treated with honor and compassion.

By cultivating self-discipline, wisdom, and leadership, biblical manhood equips men to lead with purpose, love and shepherd their families, serve their communities, and uphold righteousness. This ultimately creates a society where individuals flourish, and communities grow stronger through principled, servant-hearted leadership.

FORGING BIBLICAL MANHOOD:

An INTENTIONAL BLUEPRINT

1 Peter 2:17 (ESV): "Honor everyone. Love the brotherhood. Fear God. Honor the emperor."

The Bible—God's direct communication with man—reveals a radical plan that defies human nature yet is central to our purpose: the chief end of man is to love God and to love people. From Genesis to Revelation, this command shapes God's relationship with humanity. Jesus encapsulates it in Matthew 22:37–39, declaring the two great commandments: "Love the Lord your God with all your heart and with all your soul and with all your mind" and "Love your neighbor as yourself." Loving God with all that we are demands more than just devotion and obedience; it requires a complete reorientation of our hearts, placing Him as our ultimate priority.

And from this first command flows the second—our love for others is not an option but a natural and necessary outgrowth of our love for God. Throughout Scripture, believers are called to this radical transformation: to serve, forgive, and care for others as a reflection of God's own sacrificial love for us. Loving God and loving people cannot be separated; they are the intertwined pillars of a life that fulfills God's revolutionary vision for humanity.

Just as the Bible redefines love in a way that challenges human desires, it also upends modern ideas of honor, tying it directly to our relationship with God and others. To honor God is not just about reverence; it requires complete submission to His authority, holiness, and majesty. This call to honor God carries radical implications for how we view and treat others, as all people are created in God's image—the *imago Dei.*

This foundational belief declares that every human being, regardless of status or background, possesses inherent dignity and worth that demands recognition. God honors us by knowing us intimately and giving purpose to our lives. We bear His image and are charged with reflecting His character—His truth, wisdom, righteousness, and love—to others, pointing them to His divine authority and redemptive plan within His Kingdom. In turn, He calls us to honor others by recognizing their God-given dignity and capacity to reflect His image, treating them accordingly.

Honor, then, is more than mere respect; it is a deeply transformative posture—seeing others through the lens of God's love and purpose. By living out this radical honor, we acknowledge the divine worth in every person, understanding that how we treat others reflects our relationship with God Himself. To honor God and others is to live a life marked by humility, love, and selfless service—a life profoundly shaped by the image of God within us all.

Given this revolutionary understanding of honor and love, it becomes clear that teaching these values to the next generation is not just essential—it is urgent. Boys, in particular, must be guided to understand what it truly means to live honorably in a world that distorts the meaning of honor, often confusing it with status, personal achievement, or conquest.

At Iron Academy, the Honor Code is rooted in integrity, respect, humility, love, and courage—values that align with the Bible's radical call to honor God and love others well. This code is more than a set of rules; it is a framework for shaping boys into young men who fully grasp what it means to honor God and to reflect that honor in how they treat others. By embracing an Honor Code that is anchored in timeless biblical values, we create an environment where boys can grow into responsible, godly men—men who embody the true, radical essence of honor in every facet of their lives.

THE HISTORICAL NECESSITY OF HONOR CODES

Codes of honor meant to build men useful for God, country, and institution have a long history in the English-speaking world, tracing back to chivalric traditions, educational institutions, fraternities, and military academies. These codes stressed integrity and honesty; responsibility and accountability; loyalty, obedience, and service; courage and sacrifice; academic excellence and authenticity; and personal and communal honor through ethical behavior. More broadly, they served institutions by reinforcing moral conduct, responsibility, and a deep commitment to both personal and communal responsibilities.

HONOR CODE	ERA	HONOR CODE
Chivalric Code	Middle Ages (11th-15th c.)	"Live by honor and for glory; protect the weak; obey authority; fight for God and country."
Oxford University Academic Code	17th-19th Century	"Honesty, integrity, and personal responsibility in academic work. Plagiarism is a violation of academic honor."
University of Virginia Honor Code	1842 to present	"A pledge made by students to never lie, cheat, or steal."
West Point Honor Code	19th Century to present	"A cadet will not lie, cheat, steal, or tolerate those who do."
Princeton University Honor Code	1893 to present	"I pledge my honor that I have not violated the Honor Code during this examination."
Yale University Academic Honor Code	21st Century	"I pledge to submit only my own work and properly cite all sources. I will not lie, cheat, or steal in my academic endeavors."

Harvard College Honor Code	2015 to present	"Members of the Harvard College community commit to producing academic work with integrity, adhering to the standards of the institution."

Honor codes, over time, have drifted significantly from their biblical roots—a shift that began with the evolution of the first chivalric code. The chivalric tradition, deeply rooted in Christian ideals, emphasized faith, loyalty, and a profound sense of duty to God, country, and the weak.

As time passed, honor codes in academic institutions and military academies—while still emphasizing integrity and service—began shifting their focus toward personal responsibility, gradually moving away from faith and biblical principles. Prestigious universities such as Princeton and Yale, though originally designed to foster integrity and personal accountability, have secularized over time, removing references to God and Scripture and prioritizing individual achievement and institutional ethical standards. West Point's honor code, while still noble and character-focused, no longer carries the overt spiritual undertones of its predecessors. Harvard's newest honor code barely reflects any historical understanding of honor, allowing standards to change readily. To a medieval knight who once lived by a rigorous code of faith-driven duty, such a shift would be unrecognizable.

Harvard's understanding of integrity has drifted dramatically in recent years, as the United States' oldest university has faced several high-profile ethical scandals. In 2012, Harvard was embroiled in a major cheating scandal involving over 100 students in a government class. In response to growing concerns over academic integrity, the university implemented a formal honor code in 2015, yet challenges persisted.

Since then, Harvard has faced a plagiarism scandal involving a president's dissertation, mishandling of sexual harassment allegations, and conflicts of interest in faculty research. In 2019, the admissions bribery case further exposed ethical concerns, raising serious questions about fairness and transparency within the institution. These ongoing controversies continue to place Harvard's commitment to ethical responsibility under intense scrutiny.

Harvard's example is significant. When an institution departs from a biblical foundation and biblical truth, it inevitably drifts from virtue. Over time, Harvard has distanced itself significantly from its original religious mission and the virtues it once championed.

Harvard's Biblical Roots

Founded in 1636 by the Massachusetts Bay Colony, Harvard's purpose was to equip and train pastors for the Puritan churches of New England—a mission centered on preparing godly leaders, firmly grounded in Scripture, to shepherd their communities and advance the gospel. Put simply, Harvard was established to train men to lead their communities in loving God and loving one another.

However, Harvard has gradually but unmistakably moved toward a secular and pluralistic ideology. In a striking example, the university appointed atheist Greg Epstein as head chaplain—a stark departure from its founding principles. Today, nearly 50% of Harvard students identify as atheist or agnostic, reflecting a broader cultural move away from biblical virtues. Harvard Divinity School, once focused on Protestant ministry, now embraces over thirty religious traditions, promoting moral relativism and individualism over biblical truth.

Perhaps it sounds excessive, but the reality remains—as Harvard goes, so goes America. Harvard's moral trajectory has changed drastically since its founding in 1636, when it was established to train men in biblical truth and virtue. Originally rooted in Puritan ideals, Harvard sought to produce leaders devoted to loving God and serving others, shaping American society through a commitment to scriptural integrity. Over time, however, the institution has strayed from its biblical foundation, replacing its theological mission with an ever-evolving secular ethos.

This transformation mirrors a broader cultural drift away from absolute truth toward moral relativism, where honor is no longer anchored in God's authority but in human-centered ideologies. While Harvard once set the standard for intellectual and moral excellence grounded in Scripture, it now exemplifies the dangers of a society untethered from biblical values.

The rise of academic dishonesty, ethical scandals, and shifting definitions of integrity within Harvard's walls underscores a sobering reality: when an institution forsakes God as the source of wisdom and virtue, it inevitably drifts into confusion. Just as Harvard's influence has historically shaped the moral landscape of America, its departure from biblical principles has played a significant role in the nation's broader moral decline.

LOOKING TO A HIGHER STANDARD

Yet, as people created to submit to the lordship of Jesus Christ and to love others well, we must look beyond shifting cultural standards to a higher, unchanging authority—God's Word. Unlike institutions that redefine virtue to fit cultural trends, Scripture remains the ultimate foundation for true honor, integrity, and godly leadership.

As believers, our standard of virtue must come from the Word of God—not Harvard, not *The New York Times,* not social media, and not the cultural influences that constantly vie for our attention. These worldly sources reflect shifting, human-centered views of morality. But as Christians, our standard is constant—it comes directly from the Bible, God's unchanging truth.

1. *Before we look at the Iron Academy Honor Code,
    what is the perfect honor code for a God-honoring
    organization? What elements would it include? Is
    there one out there that is particularly excellent?*

THE IRON ACADEMY HONOR CODE: A BIBLICAL FOUNDATION

In line with this vision, the Iron Academy Honor Code is deeply rooted in biblical ideals, drawing from historical examples and Scripture to reveal the *imago Dei* implanted in each young man and in all mankind. Unlike the fluctuating values of secular institutions, this code remains firmly grounded in Scripture. It emphasizes virtues such as prudence and civility, patience and courage, gentleness and self-control, and diligence and integrity. It also challenges young men to reject passivity and practice temperance and chastity, integrity and truthfulness. These qualities form a biblical foundation, intentionally designed to mold young men into honorable leaders, equipping them to live with moral excellence and align their lives with God's standards. This Honor Code serves as the cornerstone for shaping honorable shepherd-leaders—men who stand firm in their faith and lead with honor in every area of life.

DISCOVERING THE IRON ACADEMY HONOR CODE

Does it sound arrogant to claim that Iron Academy has the best Honor Code? Believe me, if we could find a better one, we would borrow it. In fact, we did. It is not original; it was carefully assembled from an existing honor code and a well-known quote. Both were written within a seven-year span in the late 1800s by two men living 3,816 miles apart: one in the small town of Lexington, Virginia, the other in Twickenham, England, a suburb of London. These men never met, yet both were driven by the same question: What does it mean to be a godly man?

A LEGACY OF HONOR

In the mid-1860s, Robert E. Lee assumed leadership of Washington College and instituted a new honor code for all students, declaring that each young man should always "conduct himself as a gentleman." As a devoted disciple of Christ and a legendary gentleman himself, Lee understood that the Christian gentleman was the highest model of manhood. A few years later, in 1872, Alfred, Lord Tennyson published *Gareth and Lynette,* part of his larger work *Idylls of the King*—a literary effort to reclaim Christian ideals through Arthurian legends. In the story, Gareth, a young man longing to join King Arthur's Round Table, boldly proclaims his purpose for existence: "Live pure, speak true, right wrong, and follow the King." Then he asks a rhetorical question that echoes through time: "Else, wherefore born?"

THE IRON ACADEMY HONOR CODE

The Iron Academy Honor Code is a direct outgrowth of these two men's efforts to reclaim honor between 1865 and 1872: "I will always conduct myself as a gentleman" and "Live pure, speak true, right wrong, and follow the King." Now, 150 years later, Iron Academy renews this call, championing a nobility of mind and spirit built on a rock-solid standard of moral behavior.

CHAPTER 2

A Compass for Biblical Manhood

While the Honor Code must never replace the Bible, it serves as a moral compass—a guiding reference for young men seeking to maintain their course. Just as a navigator relies on true north, the Honor Code helps align their lives with God's ultimate authority, reinforcing their commitment to integrity, respect, humility, and courage. It directs young men to uphold virtues such as self-control and diligence, ensuring they remain honorable in all things as they navigate the challenges of life. As shepherd-leaders, young men are called to embody biblical manhood—a role that not only protects women and children but also strengthens families and communities, making life better for all. Just as a navigator checks their course against a map, young men use the Honor Code to confirm that their actions align with biblical truth, continually adjusting to reflect the selfless leadership and care that God commands.

> **"If you do not have a definition of good and evil that is anchored in some type of transcendent truth, you are destined for incoherence."** — Katie McCoy, The World and Everything In It, October 18, 2024

Staying the Course: A Warning Against Drift

A reliable code that keeps us oriented to God—walking the path of righteousness, neither veering to the right nor to the left—is essential to a God-honoring life. Just as Harvard and other once-biblical institutions have drifted from Truth, so too can individuals and organizations. A slight deviation today, followed by another subtle shift tomorrow, gradually justifies further compromise. Before long, what once seemed unthinkable becomes normalized, leading to a dramatic departure from Truth. Like a traveler failing to correct their course, the result is to be lost. Both Proverbs and the New Testament warn believers to walk the straight and narrow path, avoiding distractions that lead to destruction: **"Let your eyes look** directly forward, and your gaze be straight before you. Ponder the path of your feet; then all your ways will be sure. Do not swerve to the right or to the left; turn your foot away from evil" (Proverbs 4:25–27). Jesus reinforces this truth: "For the gate is narrow and the way is hard that leads to life, and those who find it are few" (Matthew 7:13–14).

A reliable, Bible-reflecting code must be central in the life of every Jesus-follower, a constant guide to staying true to God's will.

THE NECESSITY OF ACCOUNTABILITY

Proverbs 27:17 (ESV): "As iron sharpens iron, so one man sharpens another."

"Nothing can be more cruel than the leniency which abandons others to their sin. Nothing can be more compassionate than the severe reprimand which calls another Christian in one's community back from the path of sin."

(Dietrich Bonhoeffer)

While it is crucial for organizations to remain aligned with God's truth, it is equally important to surround students with a community that fosters biblical accountability. This is especially vital for young men navigating their formative years. At Iron Academy, the Honor Code plays a central role in guiding students to remain on the path of righteousness. It serves as a moral compass, a framework for accountability, and a tool to help students support one another in living out biblical virtues. The code reflects biblical standards and supports God's design for Iron Academy's young men to grow into honorable leaders and shepherds—men who hold themselves and each other accountable to the highest standards of virtue.

Outside such environments that emphasize biblical accountability, teenage boys are becoming increasingly disconnected from biblical understandings of honor. Today, accountability to biblical and traditional Judeo-Christian principles is at a historic low, driven by several key factors. Religious disengagement is widespread; 44% of U.S. millennials and younger generations now identify as religiously unaffiliated, reducing their opportunities for spiritual and moral growth through church involvement. Public education, which occupies much of a teenager's time, has become more secularized; many teachers promote worldviews like moral relativism and critical theory, which stand in direct opposition to biblical teachings. Family structures are weakening; nearly one in four U.S. children grow up without father figures. On average, fathers spend just thirty minutes a day interacting with their children, while teens spend more than seven hours daily consuming media that often glorifies behaviors contrary to biblical virtues. Fewer boys are receiving a biblically based education, further distancing them from a strong foundation in biblical values.

Masculinity is being redefined away from biblical ideals—such as humility, integrity, self-control, diligence, and courage—leaving teenage boys with fewer role models and a distorted or absent standard of manhood. This cultural shift has resulted in diminished accountability to moral standards, as young men are no longer encouraged to embrace virtues like patience, respect, and the proactive rejection of passivity—principles that are central to the Iron Academy Honor Code and essential for building young men who love others well.

Schools—whether public or private—occupy far more of a teen's time than either parents or churches and must, therefore, energetically support a family's desire for biblical accountability. Teens spend an average of 35 hours per week in school, compared to 3.5 to 7 hours per week with their parents, 1 to 3 hours per week at church, and 1 hour per week in active communication with parents.

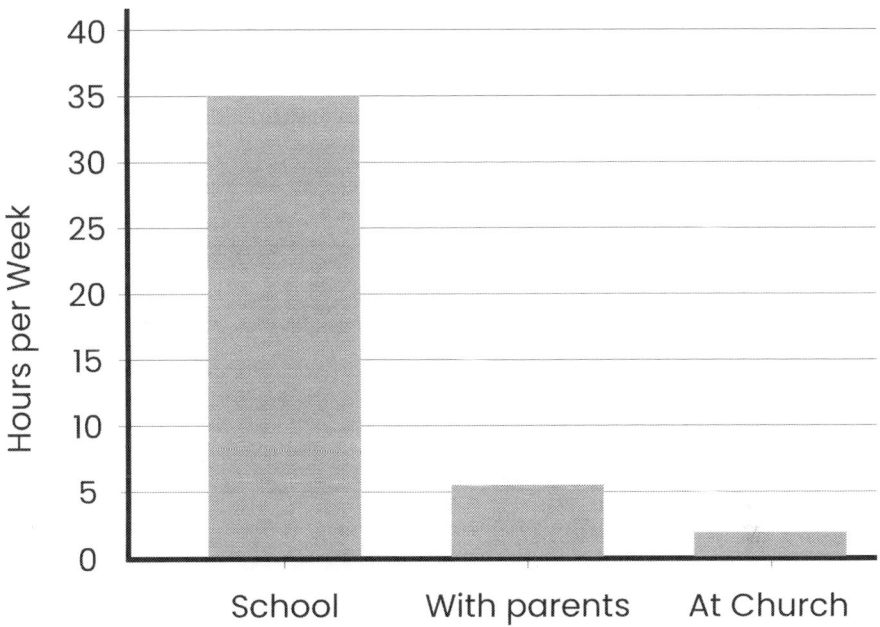

Given the massive influence schools have over young men's daily lives, it is crucial that educational environments align with and reinforce a family's biblical values—not contradict them. Schools should emphasize and support the principles taught at home and in church. Without this reinforcement, young men are left vulnerable to the constant pull of an eroding secular culture that seems to undermine biblical principles at every turn.

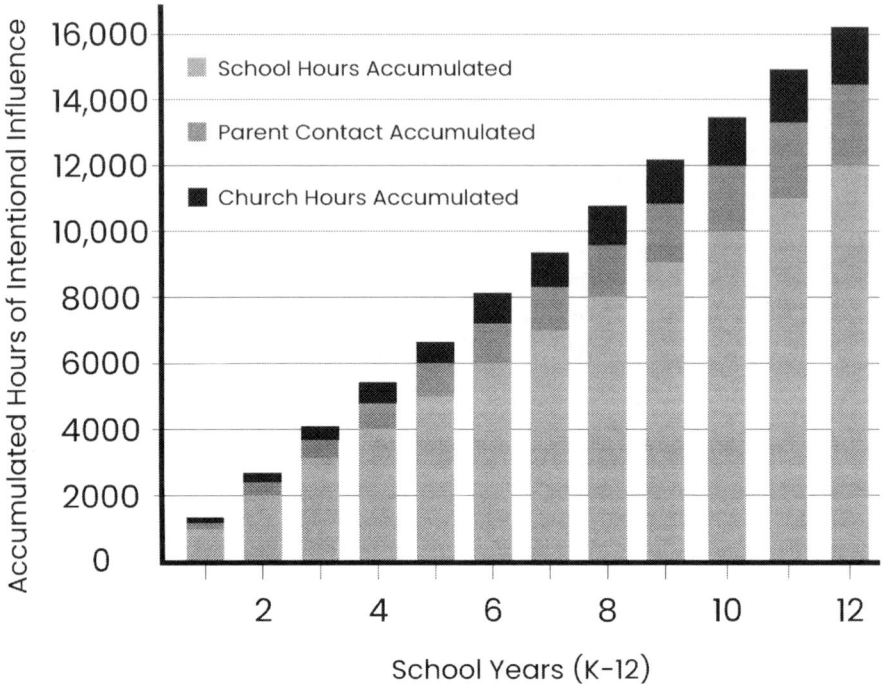

From a biblical perspective, instilling virtue in young men requires holding them accountable to live according to God's standards, while being supported by a community of peers and mentors. This process includes both encouragement and correction, with the goal of fostering growth in strategically identified virtues such as integrity, humility, and courage. Accountability is not only personal but also communal, necessitating regular reflection, clear objectives, and continual realignment with the Bible. Through intentional discipleship, young men may develop the character necessary to honor God and apply their faith in every area of life.

2. *Unpack the proverb, "As iron sharpens iron, so one man sharpens another." What does it mean? What is it trying to teach us?*

3. *In terms of shaping a young man from boyhood, contrast the likely resulting outcomes of 1) a focused, communal, and long-term intentionality on positive and God-honoring sharpening and 2) the outcomes of haphazard, accidental, or uncoordinated sharpening of a young man.*

4. *In a God-honoring iron-sharpening-iron relationship, what is the role of the older man or men? What is the role of the young man?*

5. *What does it mean to "cultivate virtues?" Is it equally possible to cultivate vices? Which is more likely without a strategic communal effort?*

For clarity, we will define virtue, enumerate the biblical virtues we emphasize, demonstrate how we cultivate these virtues in alignment with a young man's stages of development and maturity, and provide an easily emulated method for encouraging virtuous behavior. By establishing structured accountability, we equip young men to live with honor and reflect biblical manhood in all they do.

Hebrews Meetings

Almost ten years ago, we had the last bullying incident at Iron that I recall. Jon, a precocious and wildly self-confident 8th grader, mocked a 7th grader about his weight, saying, "I bet you've never even heard of a treadmill." My first instinct? Pain! The 9th-grade student leaders had the same reaction. But rather than resorting to raw punishment, we turned this moment into an opportunity for heart change and crystal-clear communication.

The student leaders took Jon into a room, encircled him, and made it clear: That is not how we do things here. That is not who we are. If he crossed that line again, there would be a Round Table with at least a suspension. Jon realized that putting others down was entirely unacceptable, not just to the adults, but to his peers. Jon had a moment of clarity—he saw that Iron's culture wasn't just a set of rules enforced by adults but a brotherhood upheld by his peers. He had a choice to either embrace it or hide from it. He chose to embrace it and make things right with the 7th grader. Jon never crossed that line again. In fact, he grew into an outstanding leader who carried on the tradition of looking out for his brothers.

That tradition became known as a Hebrews Meeting, inspired by Hebrews 12:6, 11. "For the Lord disciplines the one he loves... though painful at the moment, later it yields the peaceful fruit of righteousness." When a student dishonors his brother, he is not met with wrath or indifference. He is met with truth, spoken in love, by those who refuse to let him settle for anything less than biblical manhood. The goal is never condemnation. It is restoration. Many who have faced Hebrews Meetings have become their brothers' strongest protectors, refined through loving correction.

Hebrews Meetings have shaped countless young men, not just Jon, into stronger leaders and protectors of their brothers. Through the refining fire of loving correction, they learn that true biblical manhood isn't about avoiding mistakes—it's about owning them, growing from them, and standing firm in honor, integrity, and brotherhood.

VIRTUE AND DISPOSITIONS

Virtue is the habitual practice of moral excellence, rooted in the pursuit of what is good, just, and honorable. In the earliest writings on virtue, it was often understood as the strength of character required to act in accordance with wisdom, courage, justice, and temperance. In Christian thought, virtue aligns with God's standards, embodying qualities such as humility, integrity, self-control, and stewardship. Reflecting the fruit of the Spirit—love, joy, peace, patience, kindness, goodness, faithfulness, gentleness, and self-control—biblical virtue is more than just moral conduct; it is the inward transformation that leads to outward action. True biblical virtue guides individuals to live in ways that honor God, love and respect others, and positively contribute to society. It is not merely about moral conduct but reflects the deep formation of character, shaped by God's truth and the pursuit of righteous living.

Throughout history, virtue has been central to both personal character and communal well-being. The ancient Greeks and Romans—from Plato and Aristotle in Athens to Cicero and Marcus Aurelius in Rome—emphasized justice, courage, and equanimity as vital for the "good life" and social harmony. Many religious traditions have grounded people in shared moral principles that transcend individual preferences, promoting a universal communal good. Biblical Christianity established a social foundation for love and faith, hope and humility, truth-telling and forgiveness, patience and kindness, and self-control and discipline. Medieval chivalry, Enlightenment philosophy, and early American Puritanism all emphasized virtue as indispensable—so much so that it became a fundamental part of education and public life.

In contrast to past generations, today's understanding of virtue often lacks the depth it once had. Moral relativism and individual-based ethics have weakened our commitment to communal good. In modern culture, subjective values take precedence; personal fulfillment and self-expression often overshadow traditional virtues. For example, Puritan communities instilled virtue through foundational texts such as the Bible, *The New*

England Primer, and *Pilgrim's Progress,* emphasizing obedience, diligence, and social responsibility. Today's educational systems, however, tend to prioritize skills over character formation. Media and secular culture often promote autonomy over virtues like humility and integrity. This shift has resulted in a more fragmented and disconnected view of virtue—one that fails to bind society together as it once did. If it feels like our country is more divided now than at any time since perhaps the Civil War, this has much to do with it!

Dispositions are closely related to virtues but different in nature. A disposition is a consistent attitude or tendency that a person demonstrates through their words, deeds, and thoughts. Dispositions provide an accurate reflection of a person's character and typical behavior. For example, if someone has a sunny disposition, they generally speak and act in ways that communicate cheerfulness and encouragement. In contrast, if someone has a gloomy disposition, their words, actions, and expressions frequently communicate pessimism or discouragement. While a virtue is always good—because it exemplifies a characteristic of God or what He wants us to be—a disposition can be either positive or negative, depending on what it reveals and reinforces in a person's life.

Why is this important? Every young person's disposition is shaped over time. In a sin-marred world, our natural tendency is to drift toward sinfulness. For every virtue and God-honoring disposition, there are corresponding vices and dishonorable tendencies that take root if left unchecked. Without intentional guidance, a young man's heart will gravitate toward:

- foolishness and disrespect
- anger and cowardice
- harshness and lack of self-control
- laziness and passivity
- excess and indulgence
- sexual immorality and impurity

- dishonesty, cheating, and gossip

- injustice and cruelty

- resentment and greed

- doubt and despair

- pride, arrogance, and hatred

- disobedience and neglect

Anyone who has raised a child knows this truth from the earliest age—and it never stops being true. We are always moving in one direction or the other, either growing more sinful or becoming more Christ-like. Without strong, biblical, and consistent training, negative tendencies solidify into hardened dispositions, shaping a person's actions, words, and thoughts in ways that become predictably sinful. Left unchecked, this leads to a tragic outcome.

---

6. *Within your family, which virtues or dispositions are best communicated or are widely known to be obviously important to your family?*

Deuteronomy 6:4–9, along with the broader teachings of the Bible, calls on parents, churches, and teachers to work together in shaping children's lives through intentional, consistent teaching—instilling a deep love and reverence for God. At Iron Academy, we embrace this mission, partnering with families and churches to integrate God's commandments into every part of our students' lives, while modeling virtues such as patience, courage, humility, and integrity. Through disciplined yet loving instruction, students develop dispositions that reflect self-control, diligence, and forgiveness, learning to reject passivity, live courageously, and act with purpose. Romans 12:2 reminds us not to conform to this world but to be transformed by the renewal of our minds. This transformation aligns students' hearts with God's design, fostering a life built on faith, hope, love, and meekness. Without deliberate teaching of virtue, conformity to the world becomes inevitable. Proverbs 4:23 teaches that vigilant attention to one's heart leads to a life flowing with wisdom and righteousness. At Iron Academy, we believe that cultivating God-honoring dispositions is essential for guiding young men into living virtuously, fully equipping them to become men of integrity and character. In full collaboration with parents, we strive to help our students be transformed by the renewing of their minds—so they may fully become who God designed them to be.

Before we explore the "how," an obvious question must be addressed: What virtues and dispositions do we consider essential, and how do they correspond with the Iron Academy Honor Code? If we unpack the Iron Academy Honor Code, we find that it provides a rock-solid apologetic for the Honor Code's foundation, the desired outcomes, the biblical principles that support those outcomes, and the key characteristics we seek to cultivate in young men. At its core, Iron Academy's Honor Code is far more than a set of rules; it is a declaration of who our young men are called to be: gentlemen who live pure, speak true, right wrongs, and follow the King. Rooted in biblical truth and steeped in timeless virtues, it serves as a guide for living lives of integrity, humility, and purpose in a world that increasingly distorts the meaning of honor.

Through the Honor Code, we reclaim a vision of manhood that aligns with God's design, rejecting the cultural drift toward relativism and self-interest. By embracing virtues like courage, gentleness, and diligence, our young men are equipped to face life's challenges with unwavering conviction and Christlike love. They are challenged to reject passivity, to act boldly in their faith, and to shepherd others with care and compassion. The Honor Code is a compass—a biblically tuned anchor that keeps our young men oriented toward God's truth. It calls them to live not for themselves but for God and others, reflecting the *imago Dei* in every relationship, decision, and challenge they face. It reminds them that true honor is not found in personal achievement but in how they serve and love.

As we close this chapter, we recognize that the Honor Code is not just an ideal; it is a call to action. It is a charge to our young men to live lives of purpose and excellence. Yet even the best honor codes require tools to bring them to life. How do we forge young men who embody these virtues? How do we shape their hearts and minds for the fight ahead? In the next chapter, *Tools of the Iron Forge: Building Men of Virtue,* we will explore the practical systems and methods Iron Academy uses to forge young men of integrity. From Targeted Manhood™ to accountability practices, we will examine how these tools refine character, strengthen resolve, and prepare young men for the journey of biblical manhood. Now, let us step into the forge where the shaping begins.

TOOLS *of* THE IRON FORGE:

BUILDING MEN *of* VIRTUE

"Education without values, as useful as it is, seems rather to make man a more clever devil."

(C.S. Lewis)

"The test of the morality of a society is what it does for its children."

(Dietrich Bonhoeffer)

HOW DO WE FORGE VIRTUE AND DISPOSITIONS?

Because Iron Academy is a historical oddity, much of what we do is unique to our mission. With the guidance of the Holy Spirit, the foundation of God's Word, and a lot of hard work, we have refined, adjusted, and perfected systems that work exceedingly well in teaching virtue and God-honoring dispositions. Every method we use is rooted in and fully aligned with Scripture—designed to shape young men into Christ-centered leaders. The primary tools we use to train and refine young men include Targeted Manhood™ (a system designed to cultivate biblical masculinity in developmentally appropriate ways), I.D.E.A.s™ (methodical development and reinforcement of virtues and dispositions), unique accountability methods (ensuring integrity and responsibility), Keepers™ (instilling lifelong habits of faithfulness and honor), deep community (strengthening brotherhood and mutual encouragement), and transformative prayer (aligning hearts with God's purpose).

Sixth Graders and Targeted Manhood:

The transition from fifth to sixth grade at Iron Academy is an exciting but challenging step. A young man not only meets new classmates and teachers but also faces higher expectations. In sixth grade, our focus is on shaping young men into gentlemen—instilling responsibility, manners, and organization.

This journey begins at Crucible Camp, where our sixth graders first hear what it means to be a gentleman from the Iron Academy perspective. I've had many parents tell me about their sons becoming more considerate and more helpful at home after just that one week as an IA student. Using Targeted Manhood as our guide, Coach Mitchell and I have led the sixth-grade discipleship period and helped our young men identify tangible ways to be gentlemen both at school and at home. What does it look like to be a gentleman to your siblings, your parents, your peers, or your teachers? After coming up with a list, we push them to be reflective by asking them to determine how often they're doing those things.

For many sixth graders, executive functioning is a challenge—but mastering these skills is essential to becoming a responsible man. While seemingly less significant at first, we show our young men how executive functioning plays a role in their ability to take on responsibilities, especially in regard to civility and bettering themselves for their community. At Iron, we teach our sixth graders how to organize their binders, keep their lockers clean, use a planner effectively, and take notes in classes. By the end of the year, most of our sixth graders see the value of taking the extra five seconds to stay organized in these ways. They are able to acknowledge that these tools help them to be more responsible and more prepared to add to their classes and education.

Middle school is all about laying a solid foundation for high school and beyond. As a teacher who has spent 50% of her day with our sixth graders, it is phenomenal to see their growth throughout their first year at Iron Academy. Nearly every year, the virtues and skills we drill into them during the first half of the year really take hold around the middle or end of third quarter. By the end of the year, these young men don't just see themselves as students; they recognize their role as leaders, ready to uphold the values of biblical manhood.

(Bethany Benson, Humanities Department Head)

TARGETED MANHOOD™: SHAPING BOYS INTO MEN

Iron Academy's priority is to build a God-honoring discipleship community for young men—one that operates in active alliance with radically intentional families and Bible-believing churches. We train disciples of Jesus within the context of an all-male environment, focusing not on mere differences but on the virtues and dispositions reflected in the Honor Code. Our mission is to instill the character and integrity necessary to walk boldly in biblical manhood. From day one, we have committed to guiding young men from sixth grade through twelfth grade, helping them pursue the Honor Code to the best of their ability. But along the way, we have learned a few things.

A sixth grader enters Iron Academy as a young man who wants to please and generally believes everything his family and church have taught him. He holds his teachers in high esteem, submits to authority, and is not yet enthralled by female body parts. He wants to do the right thing, treats others well, and is, for the most part, worthy of a Challenge Coin. Then, seemingly overnight, everything changes.

THE MONSTER YEAR: THE REALITY OF EIGHTH GRADE

Eighth grade is, without question, the most difficult stage in a young man's development. At Iron Academy—and in schools across the nation—it is known as the "monster year." Those once-pleasant sixth graders undergo rapid transformations that shake their sense of identity. They experience physical changes—growth spurts, muscle development, voice cracks, and a new level of body odor they are slow to recognize, much less address. They become highly emotional, thanks to surging testosterone, and struggle with self-regulation as they test boundaries and seek independence. They shift socially as friendships become more complicated, peer pressure escalates, and their once-deep trust in authority begins to wane. They become keenly aware of female body parts and suddenly seem to think, talk, and joke about them nonstop. Their mood swings between supreme overconfidence and total insecurity, leaving parents and teachers to wonder how such a formerly reasonable child could morph into a walking contradiction.

All of this developmental chaos is natural, but it does not have to be dishonorable. Even when their faith is shaken and their respect for authority is tested, eighth graders can still be shaped into young men who live with integrity—but not without intentional effort. We had a choice: endure the nightmare of eighth grade like every other school or actively shape these young men into something better. We chose the latter, developing Targeted Manhood™—a system designed to guide students toward age-appropriate virtues rather than just forcing compliance. We did not want to simply discipline them through this phase; we wanted to lead them through it.

8TH GRADE UNPLUGGED: INTENTIONAL BROTHERHOOD AND TRANSFORMATION

One of the most effective interventions we developed is 8th Grade Unplugged. Every October, just as eighth graders fully embrace their self-appointed role of hating the world and making sure everyone knows it, we take them into the woods for the week. There is no technology, no distractions—just fire, brotherhood, and transformation.

During this time, they build massive fires, learning to cook over open flames and be responsible with fire rather than just obsessed with it. They wrestle, fish, and play King of the Mountain in freezing lake water, bonding through shared suffering. They engage in competitions, construct human pyramids in the sand, and explore hundreds of acres around them. Dads join us, and for many, this experience becomes one of the most formative moments in their relationship with their sons.

Beyond the physical challenges and outdoor adventure, the most powerful aspect of 8th Grade Unplugged is the time we spend talking. Without the distractions of technology or the pressures of daily life, these young men open up about their struggles, faith, friendships, and how they are treating the people in their lives. They acknowledge their frustrations, admit where they have been wrong, and wrestle with who they should be and who they want to be. Around the fire, tensions that have been simmering for months suddenly come to the surface, and for the first time, they actually deal with them rather than just bottling them up.

They begin identifying the changes they need to make—not because an adult told them to, but because they genuinely want to grow. We hold them accountable; they hold each other accountable. By the time we pack up camp, the difference is undeniable. The boys stand taller, speak with more confidence, and—perhaps most miraculously—treat their moms with newfound respect, because they know I am going to ask them about it in the carline. Since launching 8th Grade Unplugged, we no longer have an out-of-control eighth-grade problem. Sure, they still stink, think they know everything, and obsess over body parts, but now they are grounded in a renewed sense of identity and purpose. Rather than becoming a year of rebellion and disengagement, eighth grade becomes a rite of passage into biblical manhood.

BEYOND EIGHTH GRADE: THE ROAD TO BIBLICAL MANHOOD

Through years of working with middle school boys, we have discovered a key truth: developing the virtues and dispositions of the Iron Academy Honor Code happens incrementally, aligning with how God designed boys to grow into men. Expecting a sixth grader to live out every aspect of the Honor Code is unrealistic; he is still closer to elementary school than high school. He has not yet wrestled with purity struggles, social hierarchies, or the desire for dominance. He is still eager to please and has not yet questioned whether his parents actually know what they are talking about. But we know that change is coming, and we must prepare him for it.

By ninth grade, a young man has begun the process of "righting wrongs" as he gradually sheds the hubris, insecurity, and totem-pole mentality that often define his eighth-grade experience. He starts to see justice not as a means of gaining power over others, but as an opportunity to elevate what is right. With proper guidance, he begins to understand that true strength is not about tearing others down, but about lifting them up. Through forgiveness, humility, and self-control, he starts seeing wrongs not as problems to avoid but as opportunities to step in and make things right.

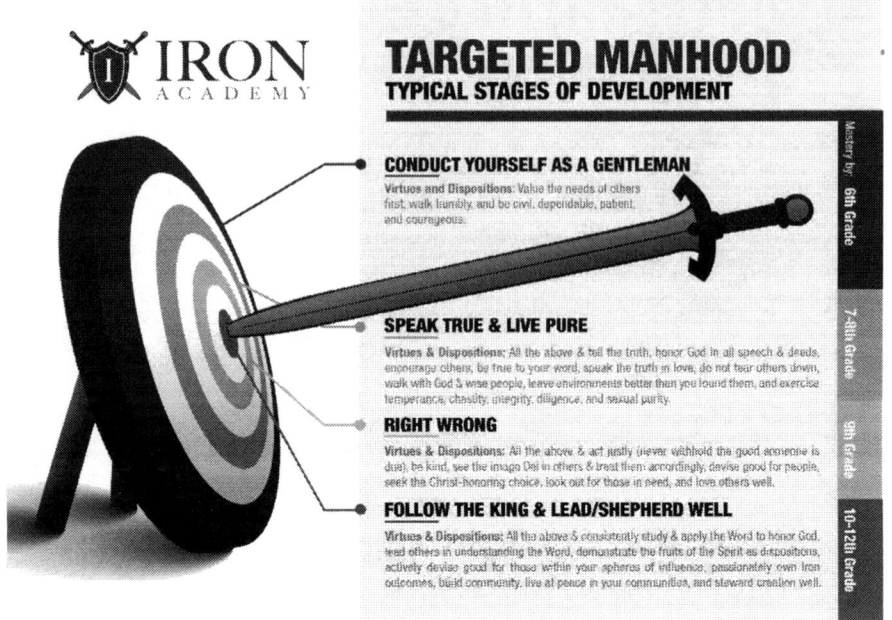

By the final years of high school, our goal is to equip young men to follow the King with deliberate intention, preparing them to live out their faith in college, career, and beyond.

The process that began in sixth grade with learning how to conduct themselves as gentlemen reaches its full expression as they take ownership of their faith. For most, their relationship with Christ is no longer just something they were taught—it is something they personally own. The accountability they once resisted has become something they embrace. They recognize that true leadership is not about authority; it is about responsibility.

Through Targeted Manhood™, 8th Grade Unplugged, our rites of passage (next chapter), and the mentoring structures of Iron Academy, we ensure that by the time they graduate, these young men do not just follow the Honor Code—they believe in it. They have been loved well. They have wrestled with their identity. They have led their brothers, struggled through failures, and emerged as young men ready to lead with conviction, courage, and purpose. This is Targeted Manhood in action. This is intentional formation. This is how we turn boys into men—not just any men, but God-honoring shepherd-warriors ready to follow the King.

Am I My Brother's Keeper?

Genesis 4:9 (ESV): "Then the Lord said to Cain, 'Where is Abel your brother?' He said, 'I do not know; am I my brother's keeper?'"

"We are all responsible for all, for all men before all, and I more than all others."

("The Brothers Karamazov" by Fyodor Dostoevsky)

When a young man has demonstrated that he is intentionally pursuing every aspect of the Iron Academy Honor Code, along with its biblically derived virtues and dispositions, his readiness to shepherd others is evaluated by staff, Challenge Coin-holding students, and parents. If the answer is "Yes," he earns his Challenge Coin and becomes a Keeper. The term "Keeper" comes directly from Genesis 4:9, where Cain's question to God reveals his unwillingness to take responsibility for his brother. At Iron Academy, we answer with a resounding "Yes!" Our young men are indeed their brothers' keepers, accepting responsibility for one another's growth and well-being.

These young men have proven their commitment to pursuing every aspect of the Honor Code with verve. Equipped with these qualities, they step into the role of shepherds—God-designed caretakers who lead, protect, and nurture their communities. The most immediate community consists of one, two, or three younger brothers. As Challenge Coin holders, they take on key leadership responsibilities, including leading their brothers in daily chores, engaging in and leading daily discipleship time together, and handling initial disciplinary issues within their Keeper group.

Ari & His Challenge Coin/A Story of Repentance and Restoration:

At Iron Academy, we equip biblical young men to shepherd and disciple others, in hopes they will become Christlike leaders. We recognize this growth through our marker and challenge coin system—a tangible reminder of godly leadership's honor and responsibility.

Markers align with our Honor Code: "I will always conduct myself as a gentleman, live pure, speak true, right wrong, and follow the King." By graduation, each student aspires to earn his challenge coin—not as a trophy, but as a symbol of trust and responsibility in leadership, reminding them their journey is just beginning.

Accountability is key to growth. When students falter, they are met with a brotherhood that challenges them to rise again. Ari's story reflects this.

Over break, Ari made a poor choice on Discord (a gaming chat app). His brothers held him accountable, and he accepted the consequences, including losing his challenge coin, as he was not exemplifying the Honor Code.

Though devastated, Ari saw it as a call to action. He committed to weekly Scripture reflections on purity and truth, reevaluated his online interactions, and encouraged his peers to do the same. His renewed devotion even influenced his older brother.

Because Ari grew and led well, I had the privilege of restoring his challenge coin before year's end. This time, it held deeper meaning. He understood true leadership is about faithfully following Christ and guiding others. Instead of seeing leadership as a burden, he embraced it as a calling.

Ari now leads by example in student leadership. In our discipleship group, we explore attributes of our Creator through Scripture. His journey continues as he grows in faith and leadership, preparing not just to succeed but to disciple, shepherd, and inspire others for Christ—a true mark of a godly young man.

(Michael Scanlan, STEM Teacher)

Embracing the call to be "Keepers" of their brothers, they come to understand that true leadership requires a commitment to the well-being of those around them—not only at school, but also within their families, churches, and broader communities. They learn that shepherding is not merely oversight but about actively adding value to the lives of others, serving as reliable sources of compassion, guidance, and protection. Through this ongoing process, they are continually shaped into young men who, while still growing, are maturing each day—developing into leaders of integrity and humility. They are preparing to make a meaningful impact on the world by following God's path and faithfully caring for those He has entrusted to them.

I.D.E.A.

Each element of the Iron Forge is intentionally designed to gradually equip young men to step into leadership roles with integrity and responsibility, fostering a lifelong commitment to shepherding others. This formation process, however, requires deliberate guidance and support to ensure these virtues take deep root. It also demands that a young man knows he is loved; none of us truly accept discipleship from those we do not believe love us.

To fight the sinful human urge to be reactionary and punitive—especially in moments of fatigue or frustration—the Iron Academy culture must be proactive and encouraging. How? At Iron Academy, we implement the I.D.E.A. methodology, a practical, structured framework used regularly to recognize, encourage, and strengthen biblical virtues and dispositions within our students. By consistently applying this approach, we create a culture where virtues are actively nurtured and praised, ensuring that every action aligns with the principles of the Honor Code.

The I.D.E.A. approach begins by *Identifying* the virtue or disposition a young man demonstrates in his behavior, recognizing and naming it specifically. Next, we *Describe* it in clear, relatable terms, so he can understand its significance and personally connect with its meaning. Then, we *Encourage* him to continue growing in that virtue, reinforcing a growth mindset and solidifying his commitment to developing godly character. Finally, we *Anticipate* its future value, helping him see how this growth will benefit every area of his life—his family, friendships, future career, and calling.

Through this regular public affirmation and intentional focus, young men learn that their diligence, reliability, and character are not only valued in the present but are also critical foundations for their ability to lead and serve with strength, humility, and purpose. Furthermore, we must fight against the culturally ingrained habit of tearing one another down, instead building up and strengthening those in our community.

An I.D.E.A. might look like this: "Bart, you have done very well preparing for class and completing your homework. Nearly every day, you arrive fully prepared and ready to engage. You ask great questions, and you add value to my class. You have demonstrated diligence and reliability. Keep that up; that will pay off in every area of your life. Your wife is going to be blessed to have a husband who is diligent and reliable. Well done, Bart!"

Iron Academy

I.D.E.A. How we daily recognize, encourage, and build young men in biblical virtues and dispositions:

- o Identify the virtue or disposition you see in the young man's life or behavior
- o Describe it in terms he can easily understand
- o Encourage him to continue cultivating that virtue or disposition to create a mindset of growth
- o Anticipate a future value to his life, wife, children, family, career, calling, and elsewhere

---

I.D.E.A. as a methodology is simple to replicate—and it should be. Young men must know the virtues and dispositions that make them valuable. Intentionally seeing and affirming these qualities on a regular basis helps us train young men to embrace God's original design for reflecting His image and purpose in their lives. The I.D.E.A. practice can be implemented effectively in nearly any setting—whether at home, in the workplace, at church, in the classroom, on the field, or beyond.

1. *How do you recognize virtuous behavior or dispositions within your domains of influence? Are you more likely to be encouraging and proactive or reactionary and punitive?*

2. *Could you effectively use the I.D.E.A. method in the various areas of your life?*

THE ROUND TABLE

Micah 6:8 (ESV): "He has told you, O man, what is good; and what does the Lord require of you but to do justice, and to love kindness, and to walk humbly with your God?"

Micah's words call each of us to live a life marked by justice, kindness, and humility. Alexis de Tocqueville recognized a model for cultivating these values in the American jury system, which he viewed as a "school" for democracy—a place where citizens learned civic responsibility and the balance of right and wrong. Jury duty required individuals to deliberate carefully, fostering essential qualities for democratic life, including fairness, reason, and respect for the rule of law. For de Tocqueville, the jury system shaped citizens into active, informed, and just members of their society. Through participation, they learned how to practice justice.

Practicing justice may seem arrogant in modern culture. Who are we to carry out justice? The answer is clear: we are God's created beings, called to follow Him and obey His instructions. "What does the Lord require of you but to do justice, and to love kindness, and to walk humbly with your God?" Those are heavy words, for sure, but they are not a suggestion. We are commanded to practice justice, to exude mercy, and to walk humbly with God—all at the same time. Whether or not it sounds arrogant in today's culture, our calling remains unchanged.

While medieval knights gathered at their Round Table to uphold chivalric virtues and dispense justice, Iron Academy's Round Table serves a similar purpose for today's warriors of faith. Reserved for egregious or frequent violations of the Honor Code, the Round Table gathers students, mentors, and leaders to address serious issues with gravity and purpose. Like the original jury system, it serves as an intentional forum where young men learn to "do justice" and "love kindness" in their community. Through these sessions, young men learn to balance justice with mercy, confront their own mistakes, and experience the redemptive power of accountability.

Among the tools of the forge, the Round Table is akin to the anvil, where raw metal is shaped and strengthened into something even more useful. By engaging thoughtfully in the disciplinary process, young men deepen their understanding of integrity, humility, and responsibility to their community—essential qualities for future leaders in families, churches, and communities who must walk justly and humbly, as God commands.

The aspect of the Iron Round Table that seems most radical to outsiders is that every Challenge Coin holder gets an equal vote. My vote carries no more weight than that of the most recent sophomore recipient of his Challenge Coin. Each student's vote is counted the same as a staff vote. How does this not lead to chaos and injustice? Because the Honor Code is real at Iron Academy; the students own it.

Just as the early American jury system described by de Tocqueville in *Democracy in America* required citizens to deliberate carefully, the Round Table demands the same. We actively practice doing justice and exuding mercy—two objectives that seem contradictory but are inseparable when pursued in a consistent and God-honoring way. It is remarkable that such a practice—one you could certainly see as a potential disaster (see vignette below)—yields unity, deep brotherhood, love, justice, and mercy when carried out with consistency and integrity.

Every Round Table concludes with laying hands on the young man in question, with his tribe leader praying over him. Nobody leaves the Round Table without feeling loved by his band of brothers and sisters (female staff members) in Christ. This Iron community chose to establish very clear guardrails, enforce significant consequences, and provide a clear path for these young men to fully recover their place within our community. The "jury" spoke both love and justice into their lives. Our deliberations bore fruit. The young men went home knowing they are loved, but also knowing the Iron community expects them to pursue the Honor Code genuinely. They left having experienced the powerful and potentially life-changing first moments of restorative justice.

Equal Votes at the Round Table?

Visitors are often surprised to learn that every student and staff member with a Challenge Coin has an equal vote in the Round Table decision-making process. While this might sound chaotic, in reality, it fosters a culture where young men take ownership of their outcomes, the Honor Code, and the school culture itself.

Entrusting students with real responsibility is countercultural. Most institutions dictate from the top down, but history proves that when individuals are challenged to weigh right and wrong, to consider justice and mercy, and to make decisions that impact their community, they grow. The process itself forms them.

This is not a system that lowers the bar. Quite the opposite—it demands what much of modern culture avoids: discipline, integrity, and accountability. At Iron Academy, young men do not defer responsibility to adults. They own their choices, experience the consequences, and understand that leadership is earned through service, responsibility, and a steadfast commitment to truth.

Yet, just as we challenge them, we also support them. When younger students receive Round Tables, they are often paired with older students or peers who excel in coaching and caring for others, ensuring they have the guidance needed to address their issues successfully. Iron Academy is not a rigid system; it is a brotherhood. Here, young men are held to high standards within deep, authentic relationships—where they are mentored, encouraged, and loved.

Mothers often ask, "Will my son be cared for?" The mentorship built into the Round Table process ensures that younger students are not left to navigate challenges alone, but are instead guided by those who have walked the path before them. The answer is an unequivocal yes. Strength and discipline are balanced with kindness and guidance. Every young man is known, valued, and given the tools to succeed. The Round Table is not about creating a harsh environment but teaching young men to lead with wisdom, fairness, and compassion.

Perhaps that is why, in an age where justice seems elusive and humility is undervalued, the Round Table stands as a strikingly different model. Here, young men learn to deliberate carefully, seek wisdom, and balance authority with accountability. Round Tables always end in unity, with the young man receiving consequences, being prayed for by the whole school as he stands in the middle, surrounded by his brothers and teachers, who lay hands on him in support. Young men do not leave the Round Table defeated. They leave loved and full of trust that they are part of a genuinely just and fair brotherhood. It makes all the difference.

It works, not because it would in every school, but because it is woven into the very fabric of Iron Academy.

3. *It is easy to imagine how disastrous allowing students equal participation in another student's disciplinary process could be. Frankly, it could be equally as disastrous in an adult community, but what might be the benefits of young men playing key roles in their disciplinary environment? Would it be worth it?*

ACCOUNTABILITY DAYS

"Accountability breeds response-ability."

(Stephen Covey in The 7 Habits of Highly Effective People)

Feedback and accountability are essential to shaping young men at Iron Academy, deeply rooted in our Honor Code and the virtues we uphold. Through thoughtful, virtue- and disposition-based guidance from teachers and parents, young men develop self-awareness and integrity, learning how their strengths can be used to serve others while also identifying areas for growth. This constructive feedback fosters a humble approach to self-improvement, instilling wisdom and prudence as they work to align their actions with God's design for their lives.

In a culture where accountability is often limited to corporate evaluations, Iron Academy provides young men with an intentional, community-centered approach to responsibility. Here, they learn to embrace diligence, resilience, and ownership—understanding that they answer not only to parents and teachers but ultimately to God. Feedback from parents and staff builds confidence, modeling civility and respect while teaching students to communicate truth with kindness. This intentional process fosters hope and humility, ensuring each young man feels seen, valued, and capable of meaningful growth.

A vital Iron tool in this formation process is Accountability Days. Two or three times a year, students schedule dedicated time to present a self-evaluation to their parents and teachers, reflecting on their pursuit of the Iron Academy Honor Code, academic progress, faith journey, how they are fighting to grow as young men, and efforts toward peace within their family. On these days, each young man speaks openly about his progress and receives affirming or constructive feedback that may challenge or refine his own assessment. This unique experience verifies that he is the same honorable individual at home as he is at school, striving to fulfill the Honor Code's charge to always conduct himself as a gentleman.

Like a master smith who knows when to heat, when to hammer, and when to cool the metal, Iron Academy's process is one of precision and purpose, forging young men into godly shepherd-warriors. Our tools are not random or reactionary; they are intentional, unified, and mission-driven. I.D.E.A. methodology provides a steady, relentless rhythm of refinement, ensuring that every lesson, challenge, and moment of correction serves a purpose. Targeted Manhood™ sharpens each phase of development, meeting young men where they are while calling them toward who they must become. The Round Table is where sparks fly—where hard questions, real accountability, and brotherly confrontation reform hearts and minds. Accountability Days test the temper of the steel, verifying that growth is not fleeting but lasting and genuine.

Together, these tools produce men of virtue—leaders, protectors, and shepherds—who are called to live with courage, integrity, and Christlike love. This is not training for comfort; this is training for war. See the final chapter for more on their roles as Christian "men of war."

Accountability Day:

One of the most impactful Accountability Days at Iron Academy involved Peter, a junior, who tearfully admitted that he had not been the big brother he should have been to his little sister. What made this so powerful for us was that Peter is an international adoptee and strongly introverted. Peter is also quite stoic in that he had rarely shown emotions, whether positive or negative. It was always difficult to know what Peter was thinking because he revealed so little in his first several years with us. This is when we began to see significant change in Peter. With a heavy heart, he confessed that he had often withdrawn to his bedroom to avoid spending time with her, missing countless opportunities to make a meaningful "big brother" impact in her life. To see the love his tiny little sister has for him and how he cares for her is powerful. To see how Peter shepherds his sister who has special needs is heartwarming.

On that day, Peter spoke eloquently and unreservedly with great resolve about how he intended to redeem the time he had left before graduation. He was determined to be the older brother his sister deserved. Since then, he has reported, with great joy, that their relationship has improved dramatically. The way he now cherishes their bond, taking time to shepherd and guide her, is a reflection of the deep transformation that took place within him. More than that, the commitment he made that day to "redeem the time" has transformed other areas of his life—he has grown as a student, a leader in school, a captain of the basketball team, and a more engaged member of his family.

Peter's intentionality has truly had its own rewards. His story is a testament to what Iron Academy's Accountability Day is all about— challenging young men to reflect, take responsibility, and grow into the leaders they were meant to be.

(Rich Anderson, Iron Principal)

CONCLUSION: TOOLS OF THE IRON FORGE: BUILDING MEN OF VIRTUE

Henry Wadsworth Longfellow wrote, "Thus at the flaming forge of life, our fortunes must be wrought." At Iron Academy, we believe our young men's futures are not happenstance, but intentionally forged, stroke by stroke, in the fires of discipline, accountability, and biblical truth. The tools we wield—Targeted Manhood™, the I.D.E.A. methodology, Keepers, Accountability Days, Round Tables, constant training as leaders, and a steadfast focus on brotherhood and prayer—are carefully designed to shape young men into godly shepherd-warriors.

Each of these tools works in concert to refine character, develop resilience, and instill virtues that align with Iron Academy's Honor Code. Through structured challenges and intentional mentoring, young men are guided to embrace their God-given identity and purpose, becoming men who live with integrity, humility, and Christlike courage. This is not a passive process. Just as the forge requires intense heat and the smith's deliberate hand, the development of biblical manhood demands commitment, focus, and perseverance. It requires a community—parents, staff, and peers—who are dedicated to ensuring that each boy is equipped to lead, serve, and fight for holiness in every arena of life.

Preparing for the Battlefield of Life: Leadership at Iron Academy

Leadership, like any life skill, demands intentionality and grit. At Iron Academy, leadership isn't just a title—it's a trial by fire. We entrust young men with real authority, knowing they will make mistakes. They will push too hard. They will focus on rules over relationships. They will stumble.

Good.

Because leadership isn't about avoiding failure—it's about learning from it. When our student leaders struggled, we saw not a setback, but an opportunity. Like in business and war, hardship is the crucible where leadership is forged. So we did what any great team does: we regrouped, recalibrated, and got back to work.

Leadership requires balance. As "The Dichotomy of Leadership" teaches, we must be close enough to care but detached enough to make the tough calls. Leaders must be aggressive, but not reckless. Disciplined, but not rigid. Our young men learned this firsthand. Some led with too much authority, alienating their teams. Others hesitated, afraid to hold the line. But through guided reflection and direct coaching, they found the balance.

Jocko Willink trained men in their 20s and 30s to lead under the most extreme conditions imaginable—combat. Even they had to learn these hard lessons. The Navy SEALs he worked with faced extraordinary trials. They had to learn the hard way that leadership is not about domination or unchecked authority, but about balance and wisdom. At Iron Academy, we teach these same principles of disciplined leadership—but we do it earlier, forging these lessons in teenage years so that by the time they are facing life's greater trials in their 20s and 30s, they will be much more prepared to embrace them and handle them in God-honoring ways. This training wasn't about breaking them down— it was about sharpening them. A leader must own everything in their world, yet empower others to rise. They must stand firm, but also bend when wisdom dictates. The best leaders embrace failure because they understand its hidden gift: resilience.

At Iron Academy, we refuse to let these lessons wait until adulthood. These young men are being forged now, so they can lead with wisdom, love, and conviction in a world that desperately needs them. But let it be known: student leadership roles are always held by our high school young men—those who have demonstrated readiness for the responsibility and the capacity to shepherd younger students lovingly. And for every step they take, they are surrounded by mentors who believe in them, guide them, and ensure they lead with both strength and compassion.

Because that's what leaders do. Stumbled? Good. Now rise.

(Coach Jon Mitchell, Athletic Director)

As these young men step into the forge, they begin to see that their strength is not meant for themselves alone, but for the glory of God and the benefit of others. Their journey is one of transformation, where rough edges are smoothed, weaknesses are strengthened, and their identity as men of God is sharpened and solidified.

This chapter lays the groundwork for understanding the essential tools we use to prepare boys for manhood. But the forge is only part of the process. The next chapter explores another vital element in their journey: Rites of Passage. These milestones are where the lessons learned in the forge are tested, proven, and celebrated. They are the moments when young men step out of the fires and take their place in the world as confident, God-honoring leaders. Let us continue to build with purpose and urgency, shaping these young men into who God has called them to be. For the battle is real, the stakes are high, and the time is now.

RITES *of* PASSAGE

James 1:12 (ESV): "Blessed is the man who remains steadfast under trial, for when he has stood the test he will receive the crown of life, which God has promised to those who love him."

THE HISTORICAL NECESSITY OF RITES OF PASSAGE

At Iron Academy, we hold young men to a much higher standard than the bare minimum of simply avoiding trouble. Society often defines success as: don't do drugs, don't get a girl pregnant, get good grades, go to church, get into college, and don't waste your life gaming as a keyboard warrior or falling into the growing category of NEETs (young adults who are Not in Education, Employment, or Training). These are low-bar expectations—but they alone do not shape God-honoring men.

We are calling them to something greater: to become men of character, integrity, and faith. Remember the lesson of the two swords. We are not settling for what is merely acceptable; we are striving to reveal all that God has called them to be.

> **Romans 12:1–2 (ESV): "Present your bodies as a living sacrifice, holy and acceptable to God, which is your spiritual worship. Do not be conformed to this world, but be transformed by the renewal of your mind, that by testing you may discern what is the will of God, what is good and acceptable and perfect."**

God's call to action through Paul in Romans 12:1–2 is authoritative, not suggestive: resist worldly conformity, be transformed, and be tested. Becoming a God-honoring man is not merely a biological inevitability but a transformative journey requiring intentional direction, courage, and resolve.

For centuries, societies across the world recognized that boys needed a structured, deeply meaningful process to guide them from dependence to responsibility, from self-interest to sacrificial service. These cultures understood what we must reclaim in our own country: manhood does not just happen—it must be forged. It must be built through purposeful rites of passage that instill strength, honor, and a sense of duty to something greater than oneself.

History is rich with examples of rites of passage that called boys to prove themselves, confront their fears, and step into the roles their communities expected of them as men. In the Luiseño tribe of California, boys lay on beds of red ants, enduring the searing pain as a mark of resilience. The Maasai of Africa required boys to face a lion with nothing but a spear in hand—a demonstration of true courage in the face of mortal danger. Ethiopian Hamar boys had to master the strength and skill needed to cross the backs of livestock, symbolizing their readiness to face challenges with agility and control. In the Satere-Mawe tribe of the Amazon, boys placed their hands into gloves filled with bullet ants, enduring some of the most excruciating stings in the animal kingdom for up to ten minutes. The venom sent waves of intense burning pain, causing trembling, temporary paralysis, and unimaginable suffering—all while requiring them to show no weakness.

Even in gentler rites, like the Jewish bar mitzvah, boys are led into a momentous encounter with their new responsibilities, standing before their community with the weight of manhood on their shoulders. Similarly, in some Hispanic cultures, a *quinceañero* or *fiesta de los quince años* is a new phenomenon celebrating a young man's transition to adulthood with a formal ceremony, family blessings, and often a symbolic act of responsibility. In South Korea, Seijin Shiki (Coming of Age Day) marks the passage into adulthood at age 19, often accompanied by traditional ceremonies and personal declarations of maturity. Similarly, the United States, earning the Eagle Scout rank requires young men to demonstrate leadership, service, and perseverance, embodying the values of adulthood. Likewise, military boot camps and fraternity initiation rites continue to serve as modern Western tests of endurance, discipline, and personal transformation.

These rites of passage were more than just physical tests—they were sacred rituals, deeply embedded in a nurturing process that imparted the values, ethics, and duties defining manhood within that culture. They sent a clear message to a boy: "You can't stay a boy. If you're going to be a man in our community, this is how it begins. This is what we expect from you. Do it and become one of us. Otherwise, you will face shame or banishment."

As anthropologist David Gilmore noted, the transition from boyhood to manhood is a "step-by-step sequence of growth," shaping a boy's mind, spirit, and purpose into that of a man. Through these intentional processes, societies ensured that each new generation of men would embody the convictions, honor, and resilience essential to their community's survival and strength.

In every lasting culture, rites of passage unfold in three stages: separation, transition, and reincorporation. The initiate is separated from his former self, leaving behind the dependency and self-focus of boyhood. In the liminal (transitional) phase, he is shaped and tested, often through trials that demand endurance, pain, and sacrifice. Here, he learns what it truly means to serve the public good, to stand for something greater than his own comfort or pleasure. In the final stage, reincorporation, the boy returns to his community—no longer a child, but a man, ready to protect, provide, and lead.

But in modern America, we have too often abandoned these rites, leaving boys adrift without a compass to guide them. Our sons are growing up in a world where the values that define manhood have been forgotten or obscured. Without purposeful guidance, boys are left to define manhood for themselves, leading too many toward shallow symbols of masculinity— violence, wealth, and social status—rather than the enduring virtues of courage, sacrifice, and service. As a result, we see churches struggling to retain men, families suffering under the burden of absent fathers, and young men uncertain of their role in society. This generation is crying out for direction, and we, as a nation and as a Christian community, must answer that call.

1. *What are the historical reasons for a culture practicing rites of passage?*

2. *What are the downsides of a culture that does not practice rites of passage for males?*

Richard Rohr speaks to this grave issue, observing that a society without meaningful rites of passage leaves youth in a "disenchanted universe." Without these sacred traditions, young men lack the purposeful connection that defines their place in God's plan. They grow up without the guidance that initiates them into a life of meaning and faith, without the rituals that bind them to community and responsibility. As a result, they pass from childhood without direction and enter adulthood without purpose.

What consequences should we expect in a culture where intentional rites of passage no longer usher boys into an intentional, clearly defined manhood that serves our society well? Consider this: What does modern American early-adult maleness look like today? In many cases, we see fragile relationships, addictive and escapist behaviors, and moral ambiguity. Identity confusion and a lack of purpose are prevalent, along with emotional and mental health challenges that hinder growth. Delayed maturity and poor leadership skills often result in a generation unprepared for the responsibilities of adulthood. There is also a growing alienation from faith and difficulty navigating gender roles, leaving many young men struggling with a lack of resilience. They are highly susceptible to negative influences and unprepared for fatherhood, while the erosion of honor and virtue becomes more evident. These patterns are not only indicative of personal struggles but reflect a broader societal issue that lacks a foundation for healthy, purposeful manhood.

The absence of meaningful rites of passage for young men produces troubled boys who grow into troubled adult males—a reality supported by history, sociology, psychology, and cultural trends. Historically, societies with structured rites of passage—such as the Maasai lion hunt or the Jewish bar mitzvah—produced men with clear roles, resilience, and purpose. In contrast, cultures lacking these mechanisms often faced identity crises and decline.

Structured rites of passage are essential for guiding boys into responsible manhood, shaping their character, and reinforcing societal stability. Sociological research, including David Gilmore's *Manhood in the Making*, shows that structured transitions help instill values and leadership, whereas their absence correlates with rising fatherlessness, disengagement, and community instability. Psychological studies link delayed independence and emotional struggles, such as the "failure to launch" phenomenon, to the lack of structured life transitions. Rising addiction rates, mental health crises, and the erosion of marriage and fatherhood reflect the void left by unstructured boyhoods. Anthropologists have long observed that nearly all successful cultures relied on rites of passage to transfer identity, skills, and responsibility. Modern indicators—such as increased suicide rates and declining male church engagement—underscore the severe consequences of neglecting these essential transitions. History makes it clear: the presence—or absence—of rites of passage profoundly shapes whether young men become responsible, God-honoring adults or remain adrift without purpose.

One of the few well-organized rites of passage for boys in the United States is the Jewish bar mitzvah, a ceremony marking a boy's transition into religious manhood at age thirteen. Leading up to this event, the boy prepares extensively by learning Hebrew, studying Jewish law, and practicing his Torah and Haftarah portions. During the synagogue ceremony, he chants from the Torah, recites blessings, and often delivers a speech reflecting on his readings. For the first time, he wears a prayer shawl and may begin using phylacteries during daily prayers. This ceremony signifies his inclusion in the adult Jewish community, granting him responsibilities such as being counted in a prayer quorum and participating in Torah readings. Following the religious observance, families host a celebratory meal or party, and many boys undertake a mitzvah project, reflecting their new role as responsible members of their community. The bar mitzvah, one of the longest-standing and widely recognized rites of passage, has played a significant role in preserving Jewish identity and cultural continuity for centuries. While formal bar mitzvah ceremonies became common in the Middle Ages, the concept of religious responsibility at age thirteen dates back much further, reinforcing the stability of one of the world's oldest definable cultures. This milestone remains one of the few formal traditions in the United States that calls boys into adulthood with clear expectations and responsibilities.

As Christians in the United States, we lack a meaningful and transformative process to mark the transition from boyhood to God-honoring manhood. While some traditions, such as mainline Christian confirmation classes, may appear to function as rites of passage, they often fall short of fulfilling this role. Confirmation includes elements like preparation, public affirmation, and community recognition, but it lacks the depth and transformative power found in true rites of passage. There is no clear distinction in the preparation for boys versus girls, failing to address the unique challenges and responsibilities of biblical manhood. The process is rarely perceived as monumental, and ongoing guidance is uncommon. Instead of marking the beginning of a journey into maturity, confirmation is often treated as the end of interaction, as if the process and personal development were somehow complete.

Without trials that forge resilience, instruction that deeply shapes character, and public rites that instill a sense of purpose, confirmation fails to define or embody biblical manhood. As a result, boys are left without a clear, intentional process for understanding what it means to become men of courage, responsibility, and faith, leaving a critical void in both individual lives and the broader Christian community.

This is an extraordinary failure with real-world consequences. Without meaningful rites of passage and deliberate biblical training, boys are left vulnerable to worldly conformity, stripped of the transformative process of biblical manhood, and untested in godly virtue.

The Old Testament repeatedly warns of the inevitable cycle of wandering from God and suffering the consequences. Judges 2:10–11 reveals what happens when one generation fails to pass down a vibrant knowledge of and submission to the Lord—the next becomes ignorant of His ways and turns to destructive practices. As an illustration, Eli's failure to discipline his sons (1 Samuel 3:13) led to their blasphemy and the ruin of his family's legacy, a stark reminder of the catastrophic consequences of leaving boys untethered to godly principles.

It is impossible to study the Old Testament without recognizing the dire consequences that come when God's people wander from His ways. Without intentional training, we invite chaos, rebellion, and the loss of a generation called to reflect Christlike manhood.

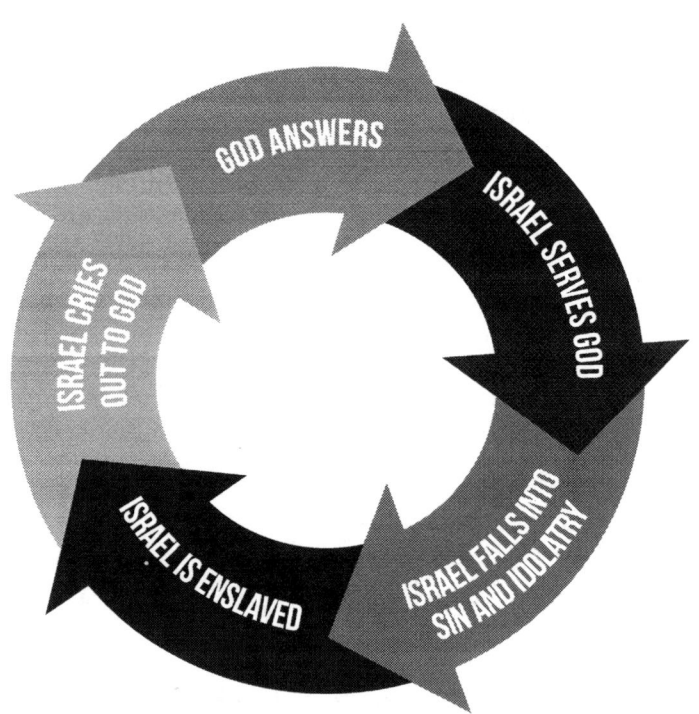

Deuteronomy 6:1–9 (ESV): **"Now this is the commandment—the statutes and the rules—that the Lord your God commanded me to teach you, that you may do them in the land to which you are going over, to possess it, that you may fear the Lord your God, you and your son and your son's son, by keeping all his statutes and his commandments, which I command you, all the days of your life, and that your days may be long. Hear therefore, O Israel, and be careful to do them, that it may go well with you, and that you may multiply greatly, as the Lord, the God of your fathers, has promised you, in a land flowing with milk and honey. Hear, O Israel: The Lord our God, the Lord is one. You shall love the Lord your God with all your heart and with all your soul and with all your might. And these words that I command you today shall be on your heart. You shall teach them diligently to your children, and shall talk of them when you sit in your house, and when you walk by the way, and when you lie down, and when you rise. You shall bind them as a sign on your hand, and they shall be as frontlets between your eyes. You shall write them on the doorposts of your house and on your gates."**

Iron Academy is dedicated to implementing meaningful rites of passage, firmly rejecting the notion that Christ-professing boys should transition into manhood without intentional guidance. Our vision is to restore the essential journey to manhood—a path that leads boys not just to adulthood, but to a life of purpose, honor, and faithfulness—a life that fulfills the richness of their God-ingrained design.

We are forging a path that challenges young men to embody biblical manhood—a manhood that serves, protects, and sacrifices; that builds families and communities; and that shines as a beacon of integrity in a world desperate for godly men. Through intentional rites of passage, we seek to raise up a generation of men who know their identity, who cherish their responsibilities, and who will lead with courage and conviction in the face of any storm. This is our calling, and this is what we must restore—for our sons, for our families, and for the Kingdom!

This chapter is a fun one. You'll learn about the best first week of school in America, experience Forging Camp and Solo Night, discover The Finishing and the most important day in a young man's life, and even get an inside look at Fight Club for Dads!

Before diving in, it's helpful to understand the names of Iron Academy's three rites of passage. In swordsmithing, there are three general phases: the crucible, the forging, and the finishing. Each phase is essential in transforming raw material into a strong, purposeful blade. The crucible is the first step, where raw materials are exposed to intense heat to remove impurities and prepare them for smithing. This ensures the material is pure and malleable, ready for transformation. The forging phase follows, where the heated metal is hammered, folded, and shaped into its intended form. This stage is marked by repeated stress and refinement, building strength and resilience into the blade. Finally, the finishing phase involves polishing, sharpening, deburring, and adding the final details that make the sword functional and beautiful. This step ensures the blade is durable, precise, and fully prepared to fulfill its intended purpose. Each of these three phases—demanding in its own way—works together to produce a weapon of extraordinary strength and utility.

CRUCIBLE CAMP: THE BEST WEEK OF SCHOOL IN AMERICA

The crucible is the first and foundational phase in swordsmithing, where raw metal is subjected to intense heat, melting it down to remove impurities. This extreme process purifies the material, making it malleable and ready for transformation. Without this initial refinement, the metal would remain brittle, weak, and unfit for crafting into a durable blade.

The crucible phase is not just about preparing the material—it is about separating it from its previous, unrefined state. It marks the essential starting point where potential begins to take shape, laying the groundwork for the challenges and shaping that follow.

Crucible Camp marks the first week of school for a new Iron Academy student. It is a week of immersion, where new students grasp what it means to be part of Iron Academy. They form bonds with seniors and elected student leaders, build relationships with staff, and embrace a level of accountability rarely found in today's culture. They are challenged to do hard things, to understand the depth and significance of the Iron

Academy Honor Code, and to begin cultivating grit—socially, physically, and spiritually.

For seniors and student leaders, this week is the beginning of their responsibility to own the school culture and Iron Academy's spiritual health. It is their time to lead, to push younger students beyond their perceived limits, but to do so lovingly and productively. They model what it means to be a brother's keeper and a good shepherd of men. Every Iron high school student looks forward to returning to Crucible Camp!

Jasper at Crucible Camp: the love and acceptance of the student body

Jasper came to his Crucible Camp timid and emotionally prepared for abuse at the hands of his peers. What, after all, could be scarier than going from public school in Europe where he had been tormented for his keen interest in dinosaurs to attending a private school in the U.S. where the all-male student body was exceptionally well-versed in the push-up, squat, pull-up, and Indian Runs? Yet, the new all-male student body was more accepting than he could have anticipated.

At the start of the week, his strategy was simple: stay away from the other young men to protect himself. If he didn't engage, he couldn't let anyone down—or so he thought. Ironically, this only made him stand out more, marking him as an even greater disappointment in his own eyes. When it came time for the big team competition, Jasper hid away in nearby bushes to prevent his being called upon.

Teachers, myself included, attempted to tell him that his success in these games was not at all important but that he just needed to be there for his team, and that by hiding away he was actually marking himself in a worse way than if he simply lost at a game. Jasper would not move.

Instead, it was the older students themselves that did not leave his side. Rather than rejecting him, they simply sat with him, asked questions, and got to know him. It was as if, for the very first time, he had been offered an open hand instead of a closed fist. Jasper came out of hiding and finished out the week strong.

Ultimately, this had very little to do with teachers or adults and a great deal to do with the love and acceptance of Iron Academy's student body and their discipleship in Christ. Jasper, as of half a year in, is flourishing. He is a vital and loved part of the community.

(Patrick Billinghurst, English Teacher)

For staff, Crucible Camp is an opportunity to shape new students, to understand them deeply before the first day of class, and to assess where each one is starting. It is an intense week, designed to jumpstart the formation of God-honoring, Christ-reflecting, path-of-righteousness-following young men. It lays the foundation for students who will one day graduate as Iron Academy men, secure in who they are in Christ, equipped to live as godly men, and ready to launch into the battles of life as shepherd-warriors.

Iron Academy's five-day Crucible Camp provides a bold, transformative, and highly effective opportunity to shape a generation of genuinely God-honoring men. For radically intentional, Christ-following Iron parents, it serves as a force multiplier—akin to adding a Navy SEAL or Army Delta unit to fight alongside family and church in the battle for their sons. We do not replace the family or the church, but we dramatically reinforce their mission, working to unveil God's perfect design within these young men.

Crucible Camp is an intensive, high-impact week dedicated to the deliberate formation of men—a process that demands much but yields more. In a culture that has abandoned biblical mandates for manhood—where boys are left unchallenged and unprepared—Crucible Camp is a return to what truly shapes strong, faithful leaders and God-honoring men. Like the refining process of a crucible, this camp works to strip away immaturity, selfishness, passivity, and worldly influences. Through intentional challenges—physical, mental, and spiritual—boys are called out of boyhood and into the process of choosing to be forged and pursuing Christlike character.

> **"I wish to preach, not the doctrine of ignoble ease, but the doctrine of the strenuous life, the life of toil and effort, of labor and strife; to preach that highest form of success which comes, not to the man who desires mere easy peace, but to the man who does not shrink from danger, from hardship, or from bitter toil, and who out of these wins the splendid ultimate triumph."**

(Teddy Roosevelt, 1899, The Strenuous Life)

From the brand-new student's perspective, Crucible Camp is a transformative, foundational experience, marking the beginning of his Iron journey—a path unlike any other he has walked in his education. Held during his first five days of school, it immerses him in what it means to be an Iron Academy student, introducing him to the depth and significance of the Iron Academy Honor Code. Through this intense week, he begins to grasp the expectations of accountability, integrity, and brotherhood that define the Iron community.

He will face challenges that push him socially, physically, and spiritually, building grit and resilience while forging bonds with his peers, seniors, and elected student leaders who guide him forward. These upperclassmen, modeling what it means to be a shepherd and a brother's keeper, push him to embrace the highest standards while supporting him with love and purpose.

Under the expert guidance of staff, who strive to know him deeply even before his first official day of class, he begins a journey of personal growth and transformation. From the fires of Crucible Camp, he emerges with a clearer understanding of his identity in Christ, his role within the Iron brotherhood, and the path to godly manhood. By the week's end, he is not only welcomed into the Iron family but is inspired to live out its values, prepared to pursue the life of a shepherd-warrior as he takes his first steps on this sacred and challenging path.

Crucible Camp is the separation they need—a moment to step away from comfort and embrace the calling to something greater. Boys are tested in the fires of discipline, selflessness, perseverance, and virtue. They learn what it means to endure hardship, work as a team, and sacrifice for the good of one another.

But Crucible Camp is more than just a radically hardcore first week of school. It is filled with team-building exercises, mental and physical challenges, firelight songs and s'mores, early-morning Bible studies, team competitions, great summer camp food, testimonies from staff and students, and plenty of fun.

On the final night, we gather for Tribe Night—perhaps the most spectacular ceremony at Iron Academy. Set along the stone wall of a magnificent lake, deep in the North Carolina countryside, Iron students, staff, board members, and invited guests form a semicircle around the fierce, ancient light of a massive bonfire.

The elected school leader feeds the fire with oak logs; the flames rise higher, casting a golden glow on the faces of those gathered—each knowing that something extraordinary is unfolding. Accounts of King David's Mighty Men, the history of ancient weapons, and a forge-like intensity of battle set the stage before each new student is called forward to enter his lifelong Iron tribe—Josheb, Eleazar, or Shammah.

CHAPTER 4

Nobody leaves Tribe Night unchanged. The next morning brings the culminating test of the week: the Trek. The young men are formed into four-man teams, carefully grouped by similar size and ability. Each team is assigned a sturdy bamboo pole, thicker than a sixth grader's leg. Attached to it are one or two very heavy stones, their combined weight nearly equal to the weight of the young men themselves.

Why two stones? Because the stones get heavier every year. They grow so heavy that a single stone would snap a bamboo pole. The weight increases because each new class enters the Trek knowing that last year's group succeeded—they know it can be done. Every year, we search for the perfect balance—heavy enough to push them to their limits, but not impossible to carry.

This challenge echoes time-tested rites of passage that have forged young men into warriors, leaders, and protectors throughout history. The Spartans subjected their boys to the Agoge, a system that instilled discipline, perseverance, and camaraderie. In modern times, the Navy SEALs' Hell Week is built on the same principle—training men to overcome hardship and instilling an unshakable belief in their own strength.

Though this may feel a little out of a sixth-grade mom's comfort zone for her "baby" boy, every young man loves the Trek. God designed deep within them the urge to do great things. Much like Gareth yearned to join King Arthur at the Round Table to "live pure, speak true, right wrong, and follow the King," God's boys were made to embrace the path of becoming a man who lives well in community with others, loves people well, and rises to fight with courage in the many battles of life that are coming his way. The Trek is an inflection point in his life that leads markedly toward God-honoring manhood and brotherly love. Indeed, this is the best week of school in the United States!

The Trek is designed to awaken something deep inside these young men—the knowledge that the mind gives up long before the body does, that strength comes not just from muscle but from will.

This reminds me of my favorite line in one of my favorite "man movies," *The Edge*. Anthony Hopkins' character is getting Alec Baldwin's character ready to fight back against a grizzly that is stalking them. The line is, "What one man can do, another can do."

This is the essence of the Trek. Each year, young men face what seems impossible, carrying burdens heavier than they ever have before. But they see their brothers beside them, stepping forward, refusing to quit. They realize that if those before them have done it, so can they. We have forgotten what we are capable of, but the Trek helps us remember—pushing beyond the boundaries of comfort, fear, and self-doubt to find strength they never knew they had. Yet this journey is about more than physical endurance. It is about embracing the path of biblical manhood, learning to rely on God, and standing side by side with brothers in Christ. The Trek is not just a test of strength, but a refining fire for the heart, forging young men into those who will lead, serve, and love well in the battles of life ahead.

They start the Trek thinking they are boys, unsure of their own limits. They finish knowing they are capable of far more than they ever believed. Furthermore, every single young man will want to come back to Crucible Camp. EVERY. SINGLE. ONE. It is an experience that marks them for life—one they will never forget.

Failure is not the goal—they are already part of the Iron Family. But ease is not an option—that would betray Iron Academy's mission and the very essence of every rite of passage in history. So, the stones grow heavier.

There will be tears. There will be moments of raw emotion—crying, singing, whistling. There will be yelling. There will be encouragement. And sometimes, one young man will experience every single one of those reactions. It is countercultural. It is unworldly. It is how you begin to build men. The Trek is both strenuous and deeply meaningful. It often lasts three and a half hours, with no breaks—except for moments when men from the community step forward to speak truth into the journey.

Each stop along the way is a lesson in the Honor Code: what it means to conduct yourself as a gentleman, how to live a life of purity through a biblical lens, the practice of speaking truth in love, and the responsibility to right wrongs.

At the final stretch, the young men deposit their giant rocks onto the mound of previously laid stones—their Ebenezer, a visible reminder of where God has brought them. The Trek concludes with a final message, calling them to what it truly means to follow King Jesus.

Iron Academy's Crucible Camp culminates in the reincorporation phase, where boys are celebrated as they return home with a renewed sense of purpose and a growing commitment to biblical manhood.

For those who long to see their sons and grandsons rise above the failures of modern culture, Crucible Camp is a decisive step forward. This is not just a camp—it is a rite of passage, the beginning of a journey that forges boys into men who live boldly for Christ. It is the kind of trial that once defined young men, the kind of challenge a man will look back upon fondly for the rest of his life. It is the antidote to a society that has blurred the lines of boyhood, extended adolescence, and left young men adrift in a sea of confusion and passivity.

This is how we begin to restore God's design for young men—by creating the conditions for their hearts to be refined, challenging their minds, and pointing them to a God-honoring future. The Trek and Crucible Camp are not just temporary trials; they are formative experiences that leave an indelible mark. The lessons learned, the burdens carried, and the victories won forge young men who will stand firm in faith, lead with integrity, and embrace the responsibilities of biblical manhood for the rest of their lives. Is there a better way to start in a new school?

The Trek/Gideon and Grit:

Iron Academy is dedicated to uncovering and nurturing God's design within each young man, guiding him to represent Jesus Christ on Earth. To instill these values from the start, our school year begins with Crucible Camp, an intense week of team building, competition, encouragement, and commitment to our Honor Code. Students learn the ins and outs of Iron Academy life while diving deep into Scripture alongside their classmates and staff. Success in Crucible Camp requires one key trait: grit.

This week is packed with challenges that test both body and mind. Field games, water games, and icebreakers foster camaraderie, while team competitions and endurance trials push students beyond their limits. The week culminates in The Trek, a grueling challenge that demands perseverance, teamwork, and encouragement, leaving each student with a profound sense of accomplishment.

One student, Gideon, joined us for Crucible Camp as a ninth grader. Though eager and biblically well-prepared, he lacked physical conditioning. Yet, he pushed through and displayed remarkable grit. As The Trek began, Gideon and his group grasped their bamboo pole, bracing for the challenge ahead. Some teammates stumbled, tripped, or lost hope—but Gideon stayed strong. Rather than dwell on his own struggle, he encouraged his team and kept them moving forward. He carried half the load for four teammates, pushing through exhaustion and doubt. With perseverance and servant-hearted leadership, Gideon not only conquered the challenge but strengthened his team's brotherhood, embodying Hebrews 10:24: 'And let us consider how we may spur one another on toward love and good deeds.'

By the end of The Trek, Gideon's beaming smile said it all. He had accomplished what once seemed impossible. His determination and selflessness reflected the Iron Academy Honor Code, proving that true leadership is about lifting others up. Now a respected leader at school,

Gideon continues to set the standard, leading with integrity and example every day.

(Michael Scanlan, STEM Teacher)

3. *How would you design the first week of middle school to optimize connectivity to the mission of the school and for students to connect well to one another?*

Just as the crucible refines and purifies, the next phase in the journey strengthens and shapes. This is where the transformation truly begins. The forging process is where raw material, once tested and purified, is shaped into something purposeful—just as young men, having endured the crucible, now begin to take their true form. Strength is not simply given; it is developed through pressure, fire, and the steady hands of a master craftsman.

This is the stage where the blade begins to take its form, though it remains rough and unfinished. The foundation laid in the crucible is now hammered, honed, and strengthened, ensuring that every weakness is exposed and reinforced. Through intense effort and skilled craftsmanship, the raw potential of the purified metal is shaped into a tool of strength and purpose—just as these young men are prepared for the weight of responsibility and the battles ahead.

When a student enters ninth grade, his permanent record begins. Right or wrong, universities begin assessing his fitness for duty the moment he steps into high school, at around fourteen years of age. Think back to who you were at fourteen. Perhaps you—or the boys you knew—were the exception, but the typical American fourteen-year-old boy is not much to behold.

Ninth-grade boys are far more likely to serve as rock-solid evidence that evolution cannot possibly be true. At fourteen, boys face cognitive, social, and physical vulnerabilities that demand intentional intervention if they are to grow into godly men. Cognitively, their still-developing prefrontal cortex makes them impulsive, prone to poor decision-making, and easily swayed by peer influence. Socially, they crave approval, making them susceptible to risky behavior and eager to avoid anything that requires real effort. They struggle to process criticism, often misread social cues, and long for independence despite lacking the maturity to handle it. Physically, rapid growth spurts lead to clumsiness and imbalances in strength, while surging testosterone fuels mood swings and irritability. Without intentional guidance, these vulnerabilities can push boys toward isolation, rebellion, or a never-ending pursuit of validation.

This is why Iron Academy's Forging Camp exists: to usher young men—just out of middle school—into thinking and acting like young men who are preparing, in earnest, for the battles of life. Men who can persevere. Men who can overcome.

For five days, ninth-grade boys enter the wilderness, where the intense heat of challenge and the hammer of adversity shape them into something stronger. Armed with their newly assigned survival knives, they confront hardship and the unknown. Stripped of comfort, distraction, and passive living, they face hunger, endure adverse weather, and sleep on the ground surrounded by critters in crude shelters they build with their own hands.

Fatigue and strain test them as they master essential skills: firecraft, shelter-building, safety and survival psychology, water procurement, knot-tying, signaling, foraging for food, and navigation.

But survival is only part of the process. Just as iron is strengthened by repeated blows, these young men are forged through struggle. They learn to rely on one another, submit to leadership, and take ownership of their growth. Though each day is packed with learning to survive in the wilderness, nights around the campfire are intentionally reserved for discussions on what it means to thrive as a godly young man. We talk about Jesus, grit, marriage, fatherhood, the hard times ahead, and the power of brotherhood. We roast s'mores, tell scary stories, play fireside games, and recap the day's trials and victories. We get to know one another in a way that is deep, raw, and real. Dads are invited to Forging Camp, and their wisdom and presence add immeasurable value to the experience.

The last night is "Solo Night." Late that afternoon, after a morning filled with wilderness survival lessons and a student-led hike through dense forest to a distant peak using only a map and compass, we take a long walk along a trail. One by one, each young man is assigned a solitary area where he will build his shelter for the night. He won't see anyone. He won't hear anyone. It will be lonely and unsettling. Sometimes, summer thunderstorms roll in. We get wet. Sleeping alone in the woods, on the bare ground, in a shelter he constructed in just a few hours, makes a young man feel deeply vulnerable.

The night stretches on, filled with the eerie sounds of nature: coyotes howling in the distance, barred owls calling to one another, whippoorwills inexplicably loud and obnoxious (keeping him awake for hours), spiders crawling across his face, and the lingering thoughts of the rattlesnakes spotted earlier in the week. Or maybe some combination of all these things makes for a very, very long night. This is a significant test.

What the young men do not know is that, though they were placed along a long trail away from their peers, staff members are stationed nearby—positioned in the center of the circular trail, ready to step in if a true emergency arises. The next day is nothing short of a celebration! As they pack up their shelters and make the long trek back, they arrive at the lodge they haven't seen in five days—a sight for sore eyes. Then comes one of the best moments of the week—their first shower in five days!

We gather together for a massive staff-prepared breakfast where the stories begin to flow. They swap "fish tales," boasting of how they slept like a rock and weren't scared at all. Or they recount how they were convinced something big was walking around and growling all night. Or how they messed up their shelter and got drenched in the storm. Or how they felt a giant snake (or a big worm?) crawl next to them in the dark. They celebrate the small luxuries they once took for granted—toilets and running water and bacon!

Though very different from Crucible Camp, Forging Camp is another unforgettable experience—one they will carry with them for the rest of their lives.

Forging Camp with Fathers

The most important moments of any Forging Camp are the fireside chats that occur throughout the day, and especially at night, as the young men gather their thoughts about what they have experienced and how it applies to their future. Given the lasting impact nature of these special opportunities, we have always encouraged fathers, stepfathers, other family members or mentors, to attend as well, knowing that they would relish the chance to be a part of such irreplaceable moments of truth and legacy.

Over the years, many men have seized these opportunities to speak into the lives of their sons and their son's peers. We have welcomed their wisdom during what we hope is a pivotal week in the lives of these young men. The quiet reflections, thoughtful questions, and powerful answers have given many fathers the perfect occasion to impart hard-won wisdom and testify to God's mercy and grace—not just to their own sons, but to an entire brotherhood of young men.

While the survival training presented during each camp isn't a prerequisite to manhood, we believe that our time around the fire— discussing biblical wisdom and sharing life's struggles—offers young men invaluable insight. They will inherit a world increasingly hostile to virtue, but in these refining fires, we help forge Christ-centered lives, tempered for the trials ahead.

I am grateful for the ironclad partnership with the fathers who join us at Forging Camp. We fight together to reveal God's perfect design— shaping these young men into godly leaders, tempered in truth and forged for His purpose.

(Rich Anderson, Iron Principal)

FINISHING

The finishing phase is the final step, where the blade is refined into its ultimate form. Once a rough, functional object, it is now transformed into a work of art and precision. The edges are sharpened for utility, and the surface is polished until it shines. Intricate details may be added, marking both beauty and identity. The finishing process ensures the sword is both strong and elegant, fully prepared to fulfill its intended purpose with excellence. It is this meticulous attention to detail that completes the transformation, elevating it from raw material to a fully realized weapon of strength and utility.

Our last true opportunity to sharpen these young men—our finishing—comes in the form of their senior trip. At first, this may seem like an odd rite of passage, but let's compare the typical senior trip with the Iron Academy senior trip.

Many schools outsource their senior trips to professional travel companies, ensuring a convenient but costly experience. These companies handle all planning, logistics, and execution, including transportation, lodging, meals, tours, and daily schedules in a "turnkey" package designed for maximum ease. Students are rarely involved in any part of the preparation. Their only responsibilities? Attend a pre-trip meeting, pay, and pack their bags.

Once on the trip, students are herded from one scheduled activity to the next, with no autonomy and minimal input. Tightly controlled itineraries dictate their every move because guides and experienced mission trip or tour leaders believe that downtime derails trips and invites potential problems. Little to no free time is granted. Guides and chaperones lead them from site to site, ensuring they stay on schedule. While this structure guarantees safety, punctuality, and prearranged access to major attractions, it also strips students of independence, problem-solving opportunities, decision-making experiences, and, ultimately, the greatest opportunities to learn.

Parents often pay exorbitant fees for this "all-inclusive" experience, yet students are shielded from logistical stress and decision-making, leaving them to simply "show up and follow along." That is not the Iron Academy way.

At Iron Academy, the senior trip is not just a getaway—it is a "finishing" experience, where young men take full ownership of the process from start to finish. The Iron mantra, "If the students can do it, have them do it," drives this approach.

Planning begins early. By ninth grade, students begin researching potential destinations using a decision matrix that evaluates cost and budgeting, travel logistics and safety, service opportunities, and direct flight availability. After narrowing down their options, students make the final destination decision themselves, learning to balance risk, reward, and reality. Once the destination is set, the real work begins.

The trip is divided into "zones of ownership," where students manage every critical aspect, including walkability analysis of their chosen city, organizing the "Hire a Senior" fundraiser to finance the trip, tracking finances and setting firm budget deadlines, and coordinating passports, visas, and travel documentation. The sophomores and juniors just learned how to make pizza from scratch from a gifted local pizza shop owner in preparation for selling Friday-night pizzas to our school neighbors.

Beyond preparation, students take full responsibility for the logistics on the ground—booking flights, arranging lodging, and navigating public transportation like subways, buses, and trains. Every detail is handled by the young men themselves, ensuring they leave Iron Academy not only as graduates but as capable, self-sufficient leaders.

Unlike traditional senior trips, where students are merely along for the ride, Iron students are active decision-makers and problem-solvers. They are responsible for navigating itineraries, handling currency exchanges, setting up SIM cards, and communicating directly with hosts and vendors.

Mistakes are expected and embraced as part of the learning process. One young man, for instance, froze in "analysis paralysis" while trying to select a restaurant in Florence, Italy. Instead of stepping in to rescue him, we (the other chaperone and I) allowed him to struggle, forcing him to learn the vital lesson of making decisions under uncertainty. This approach mirrors the Marine Corps' "70% Solution"—taking action when 70% of the information is available rather than waiting for total certainty. It is a lesson in confidence, adaptability, and leadership. Iron students return from their senior trip not as passive participants but as young men who planned, executed, and adapted in real time—fully prepared for the challenges ahead.

> 4. *There are obvious advantages to trips that are entirely planned out for teenagers, but what life lessons might they acquire if they are coached through planning out every aspect of a trip themselves? Is it worth the hassle?*

"In preparing for battle, I have always found that plans are useless, but planning is indispensable."

(General Dwight D. Eisenhower)

By the time an Iron Academy student completes his senior trip, he has become like a sword that has undergone the finishing process—strong, sharpened, deburred, useful to society, and much more prepared to confront and learn from life's upcoming challenges. He is presentable to society. He is not perfect, but he is ready for the fight ahead. He is a man who has proven he can plan, execute, adapt, and lead.

Having passed through the Crucible, the Forging, and years of intentional accountability and training, our target outcome is that he emerges as a gentleman who pursues purity, speaks truth, rights wrongs, follows the King, and shepherds well. No longer a passive participant, he is a man of action, equipped for the battles to come. This is not a boy who needs to be herded from place to place—this is a young man, tested, forged, and entirely presentable to society.

What Only Fathersor Significant Men in the Life of a Boy Should Do

Iron Academy's three rites of passage are superbly effective, but they are not comprehensive. As the ally of the intentional, Jesus-following family and the family's church, we must never displace the role of either the family or the church. Iron Academy does not organize mission trips, though they would certainly benefit the school culture. Why not? Because that responsibility belongs to the family and the church. The same principle applies to a young man's Manhood Declaration Ceremony.

A friend of mine, Archie Bost, has been a biblical counselor for men for decades. He was addressing the concept of biblical manhood long before I even knew it was a term.

Archie is a thoughtful, God-honoring man who has helped thousands of men navigate their faith, identity, and responsibilities. He begins every counseling relationship with three simple yet profoundly revealing questions.

First, "Are you a man?" Simple enough, right? The response is usually immediate and casual—"Last time I checked!" or something similar. Second, "When did you become a man?" The answers vary widely: "When I entered the Marine Corps," "When I got married," "When I had sex the first time," "When I bought my first car." Finally, the most important question: "What does it mean to be a man?" Crickets. Silence.

Archie has never received a clear, confident answer for question three. And this isn't unique to the men of Raleigh, NC. American men do not know what it means to be a man. Nobody has ever declared them to be men. Rarely has anyone shown them, taught them, or explained it in terms they can understand.

The few exceptions that do exist rarely involve biblical manhood. Boot camps, gang initiations, and fraternity rituals provide rites of passage that instill toughness, loyalty, and identity. Among these, gang initiations are particularly effective at forging deep bonds and a sense of purpose. Tragically, however, they lead young men into darkness instead of light. But none of these rites of passage teach young men who God created them to be.

As radical followers of Jesus Christ—the Author and Perfecter of Our Faith, the Good Shepherd, the King of Kings, the Lord of Lords, the Way, the Truth, and the Life, the Light of the World, the True Vine, the Chief Cornerstone, the Rock, the Alpha and the Omega, the Lion of the Tribe of Judah, the Righteous Judge, the Prince of Peace, the Son of David, the Head of the Church—we must do better.

We must have fathers or meaningful, godly men who prepare our boys for biblical manhood, who declare them to be men, and who continue to invest in them long after that declaration.

A CALL TO FATHERS: DECLARE YOUR SON'S MANHOOD WITH PURPOSE AND POWER

Every boy needs a clear, decisive moment when he is called out of boyhood and into biblical manhood. Without it, he wanders. He guesses. He looks to the world for a definition of manhood, and we all know where that leads. Fathers have the sacred responsibility to provide that moment of clarity. This isn't just a tradition; it's a biblical mandate.

Authors like Robert Lewis (*Raising a Modern-Day Knight*) and Jon Tyson (*The Intentional Father*) have laid out superb blueprints for ushering a son or nephew or a single mother's son who needs a male mentor, but it's up to fathers and mentors to do the work. Their message is clear: manhood must be declared. It doesn't happen by accident. It happens through preparation, intentional biblical training, a formal declaration, and continued follow-up. This isn't a graduation party or a pat on the back. It's a sacred, life-changing moment where a boy sees himself definitively as a man with a mission to live to honor God for the first time, and more importantly, he hears it from the men who love and guide him.

At Iron Academy, we fully support and strongly encourage this process for our Iron Families. Our mission is to forge young men into godly shepherd-warriors, and this declaration of manhood fits perfectly into that calling. We challenge and prepare boys daily through our own phases of the Crucible, the Forging, and the Finishing, but we also recognize that some things cannot be outsourced. This is a process for fathers, grandfathers, and trusted men to lead, but Iron Academy stands ready to assist every step of the way.

For families where the father is absent and when the mother has no strong mentors available from church, we step into the gap. Iron fathers, mentors, and school staff are hopeful that every boy has this essential experience. No boy should be deprived of his rite of passage simply because his father isn't present, even in an era where fatherlessness in the home is among the most pernicious maladies in our country. Iron Academy will ensure that every young man is called into biblical manhood.

THE PREPARATION

Proverbs 22:6 (ESV): "Train up a child in the way he should go; even when he is old, he will not depart from it."

The preparation for this moment is just as important as the moment itself. The journey to manhood requires intentional growth, discipleship, and the clarity to guide a young man toward biblical maturity. As Robert Lewis points out in *Raising a Modern-Day Knight,* fathers must have a clear vision for the kind of man they want their son to become.

This is where Iron Academy plays a pivotal role. Through daily training, challenges, rites of passage, and accountability, we provide a structured process that reinforces this journey. But we also recognize that true transformation happens through a partnership with family and the local church. Manhood isn't simply learned at school—it is forged in the daily rhythms of home, faith, and community.

A crucial part of this preparation is a steady stream of formation in what it means to be a God-honoring man. A boy must learn to treat his mother with respect, contribute to his family, serve others, work diligently, and walk humbly with God. Applying biblical manhood in every area—faith, family, friendships, academics, work, and leadership—should become his way of life. He must develop integrity, take responsibility, practice self-discipline, and build emotional resilience. He must learn to face challenges with courage, maintain a right view of work, and develop a heart for service and justice. This also includes active engagement in his local church, where he can grow under pastoral leadership, serve meaningfully, and be shaped by godly mentors.

At Iron Academy, this training is woven into everyday life through experiences like the Crucible, Forging Camp, and our accountability structure—opportunities that challenge young men to confront hardship, embrace brotherhood, and push their limits. At home, fathers and mentors can reinforce these lessons by assigning responsibilities, fostering leadership, and providing real-world challenges like planning events, managing money, or completing difficult projects.

The goal is to create a track record of readiness, so that when a young man reaches his declaration ceremony, it will not feel like an empty ritual—it will feel earned. More importantly, he will be fully prepared to step forward as a man who honors God in every aspect of his life. At Iron Academy, we are committed to walking this journey alongside families, equipping young men to embrace their calling. Together, we can raise a generation of godly men who lead with strength, integrity, and faith.

THE CEREMONY

1 Corinthians 13:11 (ESV): "When I was a child, I spoke like a child, I thought like a child, I reasoned like a child. When I became a man, I gave up childish ways."

1 Corinthians 16:13–14 (ESV): "Be watchful, stand firm in the faith, act like men, be strong. Let all that you do be done in love."

Joshua 1:9 (ESV): "Have I not commanded you? Be strong and courageous. Do not be frightened, and do not be dismayed, for the Lord your God is with you wherever you go."

The day of the manhood declaration is a sacred milestone—not just a celebration, but a commissioning. As Robert Lewis describes in *Raising a Modern-Day Knight,* this is a moment when a young man is called to a higher standard—to embrace responsibility, courage, and service to God and others. Jon Tyson calls it a mountaintop moment, a point of no return where boyhood is left behind and manhood is fully embraced.

This is a holy transition, a knighting into biblical manhood. As Lewis outlines, a real man:

- Rejects Passivity
- Accepts Responsibility
- Leads Courageously
- Expects the Greater Reward

This ceremony must be weighty, solemn, and transformational—because manhood is not just an identity but a charge.

Iron Academy partners with families to ensure this moment is deeply meaningful and intentional. The setting should be significant—a mountaintop, a chapel, or a fire in the wilderness—where distractions are removed, and the gravity of the occasion is felt. The presence of key men like fathers, mentors, grandfathers, church elders, and Iron Academy staff reinforces that this young man is not walking this path alone.

Each of these men should speak direct words of affirmation, challenge, and blessing. As fathers did in biblical times, they should call out strengths, challenge weaknesses, and declare a vision for the young man's future (Genesis 49). A written letter is valuable, but spoken words of commissioning carry deep, lasting impact.

The moment of declaration is the turning point. As Lewis teaches, biblical manhood is not just about age—it is about embracing a higher calling. The father or mentor must clearly articulate: This is what it means to be a man. He will charge the young man to reject passivity, accept responsibility, lead courageously, and expect the greater reward (1 Corinthians 16:13–14). This is a call to step beyond self-centeredness and into a life of purpose—serving his family, church, and God's Kingdom. He should also call the young man to a renewed vigor in living out the Iron Academy Honor Code to the best of his ability: to conduct himself as a gentleman, live pure, speak true, right wrong, and follow the King. These principles serve as a daily guide for living with integrity and honoring God in every aspect of life.

The Symbol of Manhood must be a lasting emblem of the young man's calling. Whether it is a sword, a compass, a shield, or a ring, it must symbolize the lifelong charge of biblical manhood. This moment mirrors the bestowal of a knight's sword—a commitment not just to strength but to righteousness. The father or mentor should declare its meaning: This is not a trophy. It is a reminder that your life belongs to a greater mission (Ephesians 6:10–17).

Laying on of Hands & Blessing – The father and gathered men should place hands on the young man, praying over him in a solemn moment of commissioning (Numbers 6:24–26). He is now entering the ranks of godly men, joining the legacy of those who have come before him. To ensure this moment is never forgotten, it should be documented—whether by letter, video, or testimony—so the young man has a lasting reminder of the charge he received.

> 5. *Why is it important for a young man to have important men who invest deeply in his transition from boyhood to manhood?*
>
> 6. *What are the norms for helping boys become God-honoring men in your church community?*
>
> 7. *What are next steps for you in the life of your son or grandson or a young man close to you?*

FOLLOW-UP AND ONGOING MENTORSHIP

1 Corinthians 9:24 (ESV): "Do you not know that in a race all the runners run, but only one receives the prize? So run that you may obtain it."

The ceremony is only the beginning. A declaration without follow-through becomes an empty ritual. As Robert Lewis emphasizes, manhood must be reinforced through accountability and responsibility. The young man is not merely called into manhood—he must be held to this standard, not as a punishment, but as an act of love and discipleship.

Iron Academy partners with families to continue this process, ensuring that each young man grows into the man he was declared to be. As our young men progress through their years at Iron Academy, they are constantly reminded that manhood is not a title received, but a path walked daily. The young man who returns from his manhood declaration must continue stepping forward in faith, discipline, and leadership.

This is where accountability and responsibility increase. Fathers, grandfathers, and mentors should give the young man new opportunities to lead—managing money, leading family devotions, or handling meaningful projects at home. He should no longer operate as a boy under supervision, but as a man who is expected to step up with confidence and competence. As Jesus teaches, *"One who is faithful in a very little is also faithful in much"* (Luke 16:10). By proving himself in these smaller responsibilities, he is preparing to handle greater ones.

Regular check-ins with fathers and mentors should be scheduled, ensuring the young man is continually reminded of his charge to live as a man. These check-ins should be intentional—times of reflection, prayer, and challenge—where the young man is asked, "How are you living out your calling? Where do you need to grow?"

Iron Academy reinforces this process through a structured accountability program, where students continue to grow in leadership, responsibility, and brotherhood. This is not just about avoiding failure—it is about actively pursuing the life of a godly man.

Manhood is not a one-time achievement—it is a lifelong pursuit of godly virtue. As Hebrews 12:1–2 reminds us, *"Let us run with endurance the race that is set before us, looking to Jesus, the founder and perfecter of our faith."* The ceremony marks the start, but the journey continues every day.

THE CALL TO ACTION

"A good plan, violently executed now, is better than a perfect plan next week."

(General George S. Patton)

At Iron Academy, we support our Iron Families in this crucial process. The world will relentlessly push a counterfeit version of manhood—one of passivity, pleasure, and self-service. But at Iron Academy, we call our young men to something far greater. We call them to live as godly men, to embrace their role as shepherd-warriors, and to lead by following Christ. For fathers and mentors, this is your divinely appointed moment. It is a sacred opportunity to place a stake in the ground and declare, "This is the day my son becomes a man."

Iron Academy is unwavering in its commitment to supporting families in raising godly men. Our programs are designed to build young men who will one day lead with strength and integrity in their homes, churches, and communities. We walk alongside fathers, mentors, families, and churches as they prepare for this essential moment in a boy's life. For single mothers who lack strong male presence in their sons' lives, we step in to fill the gap. Our Iron fathers, mentors, and staff will ensure that every Iron son has the opportunity to experience this life-defining moment. No boy should be deprived of the sacred right to hear the words, "You are a man."

1 Corinthians 16:13 (ESV): "Be watchful, stand firm in the faith, act like men, be strong."

For fathers, grandfathers, uncles, and mentors: this is the call. It's time to prepare. To gather. To stand before your son, grandson, stepson, or nephew, to speak words of truth, and present him to the world as a man ready to fight the battles ahead. If you do not declare him a man, the world will declare him something far less—and we will not allow that to happen to our Iron students.

We fully support our Iron Families. We recognize that this moment is crucial to their development as the leader God created them to be. Together, we will raise young men who conduct themselves as gentlemen, live pure, speak true, right wrong, and follow the King.

This is the call of Iron Academy. This is your calling. This is the call of biblical manhood. This is the moment where boys become men.

Mother and Grandmothers?

Mothers and Grandmothers: Sadly, sometimes you must be the initiators of this process. Please do not hold it against the men in your life if they are unaware of its importance—they likely never had this done for them. Women are far more likely to have other women intentionally teaching them what it means to be a woman. Many fathers and mentors never experienced this kind of guidance themselves, making it intimidating to step into leadership—especially if they are still wrestling with what it means to be a man.

But this moment is not just for the young man; it is transformative for every man involved. You, perhaps more than most men, understand why we need more Iron Academies and more training for fathers—so they can fully embrace their role as mentors and builders of men.

Conclusion: Rites of Passage

Rites of passage at Iron Academy are more than milestones—they are transformative experiences. Each trial and ceremony, steeped in biblical truth, calls boys to leave boyhood behind and step boldly into God-honoring manhood. Through these challenges, young men discover their purpose, embrace responsibility, and are sharpened for the battles ahead. These rites build character, instill resilience, and cultivate leadership that glorifies God.

However, manhood is not forged in isolation. It thrives in the context of community—a brotherhood that nurtures joy, accountability, and purpose. If rites of passage provide the framework for transformation, then community is the forge where virtues are tested, refined, and lived out daily.

This leads us to the next chapter: Strength in Brotherhood: *The Joy of Connection, the Purpose of Work.* There, we explore how the bonds of brotherhood and the shared pursuit of holiness create an atmosphere of joyful resilience and purposeful growth. Together, these young men and their mentors exemplify what it means to live as a united body of Christ, building each other up in love and truth.

Psalm 133:1 (ESV): "Behold, how good and pleasant it is when brothers dwell in unity!"

Now, we turn to the heartbeat of Iron Academy—a joyful, Christ-centered community that forges resilience, purpose, and unbreakable bonds of brotherhood.

STRENGTH *in* BROTHERHOOD:

THE JOY *of* CONNECTION AND THE PURPOSE *of* WORK

Nehemiah 8:10 (ESV): "The joy of the Lord is your strength."

This chapter is about joy: not the fleeting kind that ebbs and flows with circumstances, but a deep, abiding joy rooted in purpose, resilience, and genuine community.

To understand the unique joy at Iron Academy, we must first confront an uncomfortable truth: American childhood and adolescence have been under siege for decades. Cultural shifts, our collective dependence on screens, and political decisions have eroded the fabric of authentic connection, leaving a generation of young men disconnected, anxious, and adrift. While reflecting on these realities may feel sobering, it is essential. Without acknowledging where we stand, we cannot reclaim the joy we've lost.

There is a solution: a path forward that embraces the transformative power of intentional brotherhood and the shared pursuit of biblical manhood. As we concluded in the previous chapter, the journey to manhood must be deliberate, with rites of passage playing a crucial role in shaping young men into who God created them to be. But the journey doesn't end there. Even the strongest individuals cannot thrive in isolation. True resilience and joy emerge only within community—a brotherhood built on love, accountability, and shared purpose.

At Iron Academy, joy is not accidental; it is intentionally cultivated through Christ-centered brotherhood. What makes this joy so unique and transformative is its ability to resist the forces of modern culture that strip young men of confidence, identity, and belonging. Where the world offers shallow distractions, Iron Academy fosters deep, life-giving connections.

As Charles Dickens wrote, "It was the best of times, it was the worst of times." In many ways, our world stands at a similar crossroads.

This chapter begins with an honest assessment of what has been lost: the simple joys of boyhood and the meaningful relationships that once anchored young men. From there, we will explore how Iron Academy has reclaimed these foundations, forging a joyful community where young men rediscover their God-given purpose and build resilience through shared challenges.

Joy at Iron Academy is not merely a byproduct of good intentions; it is the deliberate outcome of a culture that prioritizes relationships, discipleship, and the pursuit of holiness. It is a joy that equips young men to flourish—not only during their time at Iron Academy, but for the rest of their lives.

These cultural shifts were already underway, but the pandemic accelerated their effects, forcing families to confront the depth of their disconnection. While technology can be a tool for connection, it becomes a barrier to meaningful brotherhood when it replaces real-world relationships.

Let us step into the forge together, where joy and resilience are shaped, and young men are prepared to lead lives of strength, purpose, and meaning.

THE COST OF ISOLATION

March, April, May 2020: It was the best of times for some families, the worst of times for others; a time of togetherness, yet a time of fragmentation; a season of joy, yet a season of despair. It was a spring of connection—neighbors meeting in the streets, watching sunsets together—yet also a winter of isolation, with days passing without seeing the sun.

Some families found new life in genuine, joyful community, while others became lost in the barren wasteland of digital immersion. For some, the pandemic was a crucible, refining relationships as shared meals were cooked from scratch, laughter filled the house, and time spent shoulder-to-shoulder became a gift rather than an afterthought. Simple treasures were rediscovered: games played together, stories shared, and long walks under the open sky.

By the time the pandemic reached our neighborhoods and schools, it acted as a magnifying glass, revealing how far families had drifted from the face-to-face relationships that once unified them and strengthened communities. The choice between living in genuine connection and retreating into digital isolation had been brewing for years. The pandemic didn't create the problem; it simply forced us to face its consequences.

THE POWER OF INTENTIONAL BROTHERHOOD

At Iron Academy, community is not an abstract concept—it is the workshop where young men are forged into men. This intentional brotherhood fosters growth in character and faith, providing a space where young men embrace the joy and benefit of knowing who they are in Christ and discovering their God-given purpose. The next chapters explore the two facets of Iron Academy's community: joyful community, which focuses on relationships, brotherhood, and spiritual growth; and working community, which emphasizes purposeful engagement, responsibility, and resilience.

THE FIGHT FOR FUTURE GENERATIONS

For parents or grandparents of young boys considering Iron Academy, know this: your son or grandson is not too young for this battle. The world isn't waiting until he's older to shape his values and identity. The question is: will he be molded by a passive culture or by an intentional brotherhood that sharpens him for God's purpose? If you seek an environment where your son will be challenged, uplifted, and surrounded by men who call him to a higher standard, the fight begins now.

For Christ-following warriors from the Baby Boomer and Gen X generations, this is the time to rise. Today's young men don't know the community you once had—the joy of growing up in a world where faith, family, and friendship were non-negotiable. This loss isn't just theirs; it's a loss for our nation. A nation without strong men cannot stand. The fight isn't over. Will we mentor, support, and invest in this generation? Will we help restore what has been stolen?

THE LEGACY WE LEAVE

A generation is shaped by the voices that guide it. What will our legacy be? Will it be one of faith, courage, and sacrifice, or one of passivity? A young man's strength doesn't come from self-discovery alone—it is built upon the wisdom of those who came before him. Our community's investment in young men today will echo into eternity. We must stand boldly, speak truth, and invest in them so they grow into leaders who carry forth the light of Christ. If we don't act, we risk leaving behind a world where joy, brotherhood, and faith are mere memories rather than realities.

If we want to reclaim this generation, we must take action: one real conversation, one shared adventure, one intentional act of brotherhood at a time. Ready? Here's how we do it.

More Than a Song: Living 'Lean on Me':

We often sing "Lean on Me" at Iron, and Round Tables are one of the best ways to reflect the lyrics of this song. Yes, it's a tall order to ask a young man to stand in front of all of his peers and admit his wrongdoings. But oh, the reward that follows when brothers are given the space to support one another is immeasurable! Round Tables exist to provoke heart-change in the young man being held accountable, reinforcing Iron Academy's commitment to brotherhood and growth. They are public proceedings for the Iron students and staff to address a repeated or gross disregard for the Honor Code.

One such moment occurred when a student was brought to a Round Table after repeatedly pilfering snacks from his peers. Understandably, his Iron brothers were frustrated by his actions, feeling the sting of repeated offenses. However, during the Round Table's time for conversation, reflection, and accountability, their hearts softened. The young man tearfully opened up about a medical allergy that required him to maintain a strict diet. He confessed that he often craved the food his peers enjoyed and found himself giving in to temptation to steal, just to experience more flavorful, "normal" food. Standing before his Iron family, he admitted his struggle and humbly asked for their help, recognizing he could not overcome it alone.

After deliberating in tribes, not only were appropriate consequences determined, but more importantly, proactive guardrails were put in place to support him. Multiple peers volunteered to buddy up with him at lunch. The student body agreed to prioritize keeping their snacks out of sight to help their brother resist temptation. But the most beautiful moment came when the entire group gathered to pray over him. Round Tables always conclude with prayer led by a student's keeper or leader, but this time, peer after peer stepped forward to pray for their brother. The camaraderie and compassion in their voices moved many to tears. The student body and staff encircled him, laid hands on his head and shoulders, and prayed directly for him. They genuinely cared for their brother's heart and longed to see his life changed and healed by Jesus. In that moment, the lyrics of 'Lean on Me' came to life—not just in song, but in action, as he leaned on his brothers and, most importantly, on Christ.

This young man has since grown into an excellent tribe leader. I fully believe that the sharpening he received during that Round Table was a watershed moment in his life, showing him what it truly means to lean on his Iron family and, most importantly, on Jesus.

(Bethany Benson, Humanities Department Head)

THE FORGE
of JOY AND PURPOSE:
PART ONE – JOYFUL COMMUNITY

Proverbs 17:17 (ESV): "A friend loves at all times, and a brother is born for adversity."

Iron Academy creates an environment where young men rediscover the joy of connection and purpose across four primary areas. First, research consistently shows that environments rooted in clear moral frameworks provide stability, safety, and even joy. Adolescents with a defined set of values are less likely to experience anxiety and more likely to develop resilience and purpose. A 2020 study in Child Development found that young people with a strong moral foundation are better equipped to navigate challenges, build stable relationships, and achieve academic success. Similarly, Pew Research Center data highlights that individuals adhering to a faith-based moral code report greater life satisfaction and emotional well-being. This clarity acts as an anchor in a world of shifting norms, giving young men confidence and security as they face life's complexities.

1. *How has the digital world affected the quality of friendships for young people? How are digital worlds affecting the quality of adult friendships?*

2. *Why would limiting digital exposure—social media, video gaming, digital binging—prior to a teen earning his/her driver's license positively affect a young person's development?*

At Iron Academy, the Honor Code embodies this clarity, instilling virtues like integrity, humility, and respect, as discussed earlier. These principles create an environment where young men learn that moral certainty is not a limitation but a source of empowerment. Research supports this: schools emphasizing character education often report fewer behavioral issues and stronger interpersonal relationships among students. By aligning their actions with God's unchanging truth, young men discover that integrity builds trust and purpose, enabling them to navigate relationships and decisions with confidence.

I Am My Brother's Keeper:

One of the greatest reassurances a person can have is knowing that someone has your back. The prevailing spirit of the age is self-preservation, and we are taught to celebrate pushing our way to the front of the line, leaving others in our wake. I am proud to say that is not the way things are done at Iron Academy.

We have an expression here to remind us of this: "I am my brother's keeper!" In Genesis 4:9, God asks Cain what happened to his brother, Abel. Cain replies with indifference and is met with God's justice. We at Iron Academy unashamedly affirm that we are indeed our brother's keeper. Students find it encouraging to be part of a culture that looks out for and cares for one another.

But this call is also a challenge—not just to receive support, but to give it. This is difficult. It requires grit. You must fight. That is what we do here: we fight for one another as we all fight to follow the King.

It is my blessing to see students live out this principle on their own. For many of them, it has become second nature. Within weeks of becoming students at Iron Academy, I have even seen sixth graders hold their brothers accountable, offering either encouragement or reproof for their effort in class or their conduct. One sixth grader offered to help his classmate when he had to use crutches for a fractured hip. Every day, he carried his classmate's bag for him to class and to his locker. The injured classmate kindly accepted this brotherly act of love.

The world might admire this kind of kindness, but in most cases, it fades over time. The injured student surely appreciated the help but still desired some independence. At the same time, his helper may not have initially realized the weight of such a commitment. This is often true of adults. However, these two sixth graders made a commitment to being the other's keeper. They held each other up in brotherly love. Most importantly, they fought for each other.

This is what makes Iron Academy different. Here, we do not walk alone. We fight for each other because that is what brothers do.

(Josh Manley, History Teacher)

This foundation of moral clarity also offers true freedom. Rooted in Scripture, young men learn that freedom isn't about chasing every impulse but about living in alignment with God's design. Studies in the American Journal of Psychiatry show that adolescents with a clear moral framework are less prone to depression and anxiety, with faith equipping them to handle stress and uncertainty better than peers without such clarity.

At Iron Academy, young men embrace this truth, finding joy in standing firm on eternal principles that guide them toward a life of purpose and fulfillment.

Second, Iron Academy intentionally partners with deeply committed parents who share a clear vision for their sons' development. Recognizing parents as the primary shepherds, Iron Academy doesn't replace their role but reinforces it. This partnership is vital to the discipleship process, ensuring that values instilled at home align with the school environment. By collaborating with families invested in their sons' character and faith, Iron Academy builds a unified, intentional community that nurtures young men into strong, principled leaders.

Research highlights the profound impact of parental involvement on a child's spiritual, emotional, and academic growth. Studies show that children with engaged parents are more likely to excel academically, build strong relationships, and develop a clear sense of identity. When home, school, and church align, they create a stable foundation, equipping young men to thrive in all areas of life.

To support this partnership, Iron Academy equips parents with tools like Accountability Days and the I.D.E.A. methodology, empowering them to reinforce the school's culture of encouragement and accountability at home. By affirming virtues such as diligence, respect, and humility, parents play a critical role in shaping their sons' character. This collaboration ensures consistent discipleship across all aspects of a young man's life.

This unified vision between parents and staff provides clarity and confidence in young men's development. Together, they model biblical values and create a cohesive framework for growth. Young men learn they're not on this journey alone but are surrounded by adults deeply invested in their success. This partnership fosters security and joy as they see faith, family, church, and education working together to guide them toward a Christ-centered life.

Third, Iron Academy builds a culture of brotherhood that promotes genuine, safe community. True brotherhood is forged in shared struggles and celebrations, and the single-gender environment allows young men to connect authentically. Trust and camaraderie flourish as they navigate challenges and triumphs together.

Brotherhood isn't without difficulties, but overcoming obstacles deepens relationships and uncovers joy. Intentional experiences like 8th Grade Unplugged, Tribe Night, and 11th-grade camping trips in Linville Gorge push young men to rely on one another and persevere. Whether cooking over a campfire, braving cold October lake water, or tackling tough goals, these challenges cultivate resilience and mutual respect, forming lasting bonds.

Milestone celebrations, like the Challenge Coin ceremony (see Chapter 3), affirm belonging and achievement, reinforcing community ties. These moments provide tangible reminders of progress and place within the brotherhood, inspiring pride, joy, and purpose as young men see the rewards of their commitment to the Honor Code.

Conflict is inevitable, but at Iron Academy, it's an opportunity for growth. Guided by Matthew 18:15–17, young men learn to handle disagreements with integrity and grace:

> **"If your brother sins against you, go and tell him his fault, between you and him alone. If he listens to you, you have gained your brother. But if he does not listen, take one or two others along with you, that every charge may be established by the evidence of two or three witnesses. If he refuses to listen to them, tell it to the church. And if he refuses to listen even to the church, let him be to you as a Gentile and a tax collector."**

This approach fosters honest communication and humility. If private resolution fails, young men seek wise counsel from trusted peers or mentors, reinforcing the Honor Code's focus on fairness and accountability. True brotherhood seeks truth and reconciliation, not division.

In rare cases requiring broader input, the Round Table process ensures conflicts are addressed with wisdom and care, concluding with prayer and encouragement so no one feels isolated or unloved.

3. *Men: how might you be different today had you attended (and devoted yourself to) a school like Iron Academy? Would you be better equipped as a friend? A husband? Would you be better equipped to be a mentor?*

4. *Women: data reveal that women married to men who attended all-male schools report their husbands treat them significantly better and they have better marital outcomes than those whose husbands attended co-ed schools. How might attending a school like Iron Academy better prepare men for life as a husband and as a father than traditional or even typical Christian schools?*

Through shared challenges, milestone celebrations, and biblical conflict resolution, Iron Academy fosters a brotherhood where young men learn humility, forgiveness, and grace. Reconciliation strengthens relationships, building enduring bonds. In this culture, they find a safe, joyful community that prepares them for leadership in families, churches, and beyond.

Finally, Iron Academy builds a culture of group discipleship and accountability—a space for spiritual growth, shared struggles, and mutual encouragement in faith. Small, safe settings foster open discussions about the Bible, life, and their walk with Christ, allowing honest exploration with vulnerability.

This judgment-free environment removes barriers to community, empowering young men to forge authentic connections and voice genuine questions about faith. This is critical: if they can't express doubts among those who love them, they may suppress them, only to abandon faith and the Church in college.

Biblical Conflict Resolution:

As a teacher who attended public schools throughout my life, the way Iron Academy handles correction is truly different from anything I have ever experienced. Elsewhere, correction is often either reactionary, punitive, or ignored. It's one thing for a school to claim that it is centered on the Bible, but it's an entirely different thing to live it out. One example of this occurred among an eighth-grade class as they embodied Jesus' teachings in Matthew 18 on how to hold a brother accountable.

During lunch, two 8th-grade students approached me and asked if I could supervise a discussion with one of their classmates. As I walked into the classroom, I saw every member of the 8th-grade class seated at a desk, with one of their classmates facing them at the front of the room. The atmosphere was serious but not angry—there was a sense of gravity and solemnity, yet it remained respectful and controlled. What I witnessed was a loving and respectful conversation as the class collectively held their brother accountable for words and actions that had grown increasingly harmful over time. The student seated at the front of the room received the comments and questions in a mature manner and has since corrected his behaviors that needed attention.

After the meeting, I was informed by a student present that they had followed the biblical steps outlined in Matthew 18. Initially, they met with their classmate one-on-one (Matthew 18:15). After not gaining much traction, they brought in one or two more peers to address the issue together (Matthew 18:16). The meeting I had the privilege of witnessing was the fulfillment of the third step Jesus instructs—to bring the matter before the community (Matthew 18:17).

As a teacher, it is refreshing to see 8th-grade young men handle Bible-based accountability in a way that many of us as adults either cannot or choose not to handle. Their commitment to biblical principles not only strengthens their character but also fosters a culture of integrity, humility, and brotherhood within the school. Imagine a world in which adults fully embraced this same biblical model of accountability—how much more God-honoring, peaceful, and unified our communities, workplaces, and churches could be!

(Tanner Brown, Bible Teacher)

Mentorship and accountability from staff and older students model Christlike leadership, inspiring younger men to deepen their faith and relationships. Through consistent guidance, Iron students learn accountability's role in spiritual and personal growth, challenging them to live honorably and support one another.

In this environment, young men experience discipleship's transformative power, growing closer to God and forming meaningful peer bonds. Iron Academy's commitment to group discipleship equips them to carry these values into their families, churches, and communities, preparing them for lives of integrity and purpose.

The joyful community at Iron Academy reflects God's design for relationships, where connection and purpose bring lasting fulfillment. Rooted in meaningful ties with God, family, and peers, young men flourish. This Christ-centered brotherhood equips them to face life's challenges with integrity, grace, and a strong moral compass.

Through shared experiences, intentional discipleship, and accountability, they discover that joy isn't in fleeting pleasures but in lives lived for something greater. These bonds form the foundation for their growth, preparing them to step confidently into roles as leaders, friends, and men of faith.

Birthday Text from an Iron Graduate

After wishing an Iron graduate a happy birthday by text, I received the following reply. As an aside, I love that he texts using complete sentences! That makes his former U.S. Constitution teacher very happy.

"It's insane how much I learned from Iron. I may have been a terrible student [he wasn't], but the practical skills I learned there I have carried with me everywhere I've been. My attention to detail and work ethic I had when it came to cleaning, my leadership and conflict resolution skills I learned as a tribe leader, the code I have carried in my heart in every scenario I'm in... It's ironic looking back on it, how my mom forced me to put my name in on the tribe leader ballot and how I dreaded leading other people. I treasure the skills that I learned from that now, and they've allowed me to get opportunities that would've otherwise not been afforded to me."

As they thrive in this relational environment, they learn joyful connection is just one part of the journey. Purposeful work, the next step, builds resilience and discipline for their God-given purpose. The transition from Joyful Community to Working Community ensures young men not only find fulfillment in relationships but also develop the strength to live impactful, service-oriented lives. Together, these forge a foundation for lasting influence.

Julian:

A parent of a runner representing an opposing team at one of our cross-country races approached me shortly after the conclusion of the middle school race. Spotting my Iron Academy coaching attire, she walked up to share an observation.

She said, "I don't think anyone saw this but, as one of your runners crossed the finish line with a runner from the other team, the other runner leaned forward at the line and then collapsed. The volunteer handing out the placement cards gave your runner the 6th place card instead of the other runner. I watched to see what would happen. Your runner continued over to the cooler to get a bottle of water. When he looked down and saw his number, I watched him pause for a moment.

Then he walked over to the volunteer and said, 'The other runner finished ahead of me. This is his number. I finished 7th.' The volunteer thanked him, and I noted that the other runner hadn't even noticed the error.

"Coach, I've heard you tell your team multiple times that their testimony means more than their time or placement. I wanted you to know that your young men are listening."

Coaches want their teams to win, no doubt. But when we focus on integrity and sportsmanship above just winning, we develop caring, respectful young men and women who may also excel in sports. Winning isn't just about placement, it's about character.

Oh, and Julian, just an eighth grader, has had his heart for serving others recognized by a spectator for the second time.

Go Swordsmen!!

(Coach Jon Mitchell, Athletic Director)

THE FORGE
of JOY AND
PURPOSE:
PART TWO – WORKING
COMMUNITY

The Working Community at Iron Academy equips young men to engage in meaningful work, take responsibility, and build resilience. Through intentional challenges and purposeful engagement, they find joy in the process of becoming men. Beyond completing tasks, they learn to contribute in ways that shape their character and community. This framework fosters a sense of purpose, reinforcing that meaningful work is not just a duty but a privilege. Iron Academy focuses on four key areas to guide young men toward maturity and responsibility.

First, we cultivate joy in purposeful living. By guiding young men through developmentally appropriate phases of growth, we provide clear targets and responsibilities aligned with their journey from boyhood to manhood. This intentional approach ensures they understand expectations and embrace the virtues needed to meet them.

Through the Targeted Manhood™ framework, young men grow incrementally, embodying virtues like diligence, courage, and self-control at each stage. This phased approach addresses the unique challenges of each developmental period while offering a roadmap for growth. As they progress, they're challenged to reach new levels of maturity, responsibility, and Christlike character.

Accountability Days provide structured opportunities for reflection. During these sessions, young men receive affirming and constructive feedback from parents and staff, encouraging ownership of their development. This reinforces the Honor Code, fostering self-awareness and personal accountability. Through these practices, Iron Academy instills joy in purposeful living, showing young men that their efforts matter within the community and to the God who designed them for greatness.

Second, working community emerges through chores and shared ownership of the school property. At Iron Academy, chores are more than tasks—they're tools for building responsibility, teamwork, and pride in a shared space. By maintaining their environment, young men learn the value of diligence and the satisfaction of meaningful work. Within Keeper groups, this system also offers effective leadership training, as Keepers are accountable for their younger brothers' chore performance. Through trial and error and by observing successful Keepers, each young man develops real-world leadership skills.

These daily responsibilities teach young men that their efforts impact their community's well-being. Whether cleaning common areas, maintaining outdoor spaces, or contributing to campus projects, they experience the rewards of hard work firsthand. They gain satisfaction from contributing to something larger than themselves.

1. *How have societal changes in family dynamics and technology influenced the role of work and responsibility for young people today?*

2. *In what ways does the process of doing chores at Iron Academy contribute to developing leadership and responsibility in students?*

3. *What are the potential consequences—positive or negative—of shielding young people from significant chores?*

4. *How does the concept of 'purposeful living' shape a young man's experience at Iron Academy, and how can it be applied in everyday life?*

Chores also strengthen bonds. Working side by side, young men rely on one another, communicate effectively, and celebrate collective accomplishments. This shared effort builds trust and mutual respect, deepening their sense of belonging within the Iron Academy brotherhood. Simple tasks become opportunities to enhance relationships and foster community ownership.

The Fruit of Chores: Benji and Landen

We started the chores tradition day one at Iron Academy. Why? We didn't want young men who couldn't or wouldn't step into situations to make things better. We didn't want Iron students to think they were too good for any kind of work. The results are clear:

- *students who take ownership of the school's cleanliness*

- *we have never had graffiti issues*

- *we have young men of various grades working hard together to achieve a common goal*

- *they learn to be accountable for their work*
- *they know how to do things*

One of my favorite examples of this culture happened recently in the restroom. I walked in to see a rather comical scene. Two of our 6th graders, Benjamin and Landen, were standing inside the open stall and staring down into a full-to-the-rim toilet. Outside the stall was a mop bucket full of clean water and a mop. In Benjamin's hands was a giant black plunger. I asked, "What's going on?" Benji, full of energy, answered, "The toilet is clogged, and we're trying to fix it, but we can't get the plunger to work." I followed with, "Would you like me to show you how?" They both responded enthusiastically, "Yes, Sir!" After a micro-tutorial on the finer points of plunging, gently pushing the air out, and using suction then force to relieve the clog, their eyes brightened and gave off that unmistakable joy that comes from learning something new and doing it well. I asked, "Good?" In tandem, Benji and Landen said, "Yes, Sir!" Unsure of where this would go, I asked, "Would you like me to take care of the rest of this?" Thankfully, the answer was, "No, Sir. We can do it!"

It may sound trivial, but that story brings me great joy. It's not really about a clogged toilet—it's about something so much bigger. It's about young men who don't look for someone else to handle the mess. It's about the confidence that comes from learning, the willingness to take responsibility, and the quiet pride in a job well done. At Iron Academy, we don't raise bystanders. We raise men who step up, get their hands dirty, and make things better—no matter how small the task. And long after they leave Iron Academy, I hope they'll carry that mindset into every aspect of life—at home, at work, and in their communities.

Third, Iron Academy keeps young men connected to one another, the natural world, and engaging academics through low-tech engagement and targeted learning. In a screen-dominated culture, Iron Academy prioritizes tangible experiences and God's creation. These hands-on practices counter digital isolation, fostering resilience, teamwork, and creativity.

Young men spend their years here immersed in problem-solving, collaboration, and grit-building activities—whether building shelters, cooking over campfires, pulling weeds, unclogging toilets, constructing and competing with trebuchets, holding a brother accountable, or navigating Europe. These unplugged moments create bonds strengthened by shared challenges and triumphs, yielding a sense of accomplishment.

Three-legged Stool

It cannot be overstated how crucial the Iron Parent and their church is to the success of what we do. Without the hard decisions they have made regarding digital screens in their homes and their son's pockets, our strategies would be inadequate. Without their ongoing battle to keep their sons' minds pure, even in the face of a powerful cultural and spiritual enemy, our Iron solutions would be mere band-aids over a broken bone.

Equally vital is the role of the evangelical, Bible-believing churches our Iron families attend. Like a three-legged stool, each component—home, school, and church—must work in harmony to create a stable foundation.

The stool represents our educational philosophy. Remove any leg, and the entire structure collapses. The first leg is the family, where parents serve as the primary disciplers and role models. The second leg is the Christ-centered, Bible-teaching church that reinforces biblical values and provides community beyond the school. The third leg is Iron Academy itself, where we intentionally forge young men into Christ-followers who understand their calling as warrior-shepherds.

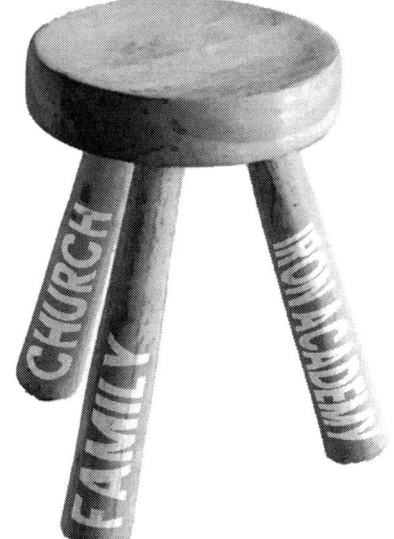

When all three legs work in unison, young men receive consistent messages about their identity, purpose, and responsibilities as godly men. Their faith isn't compartmentalized but integrated into every aspect of life. The church provides theological foundation, the home offers practical application, and Iron Academy creates a brotherhood that challenges and strengthens.

This three-legged structure isn't merely philosophical—it's biblical. Moses instructed parents to teach God's commands diligently to their children "when you sit in your house, and when you walk by the way, and when you lie down, and when you rise" (Deuteronomy 6:7). The community of faith reinforced these lessons through celebrations, sacrifices, and corporate worship. The educational structure (whether formal or apprenticeship) equipped young people with the skills needed to fulfill their calling.

At Iron Academy, we recognize we are merely one leg of this vital structure. We don't pretend to be the complete solution. Rather, we're committed to strengthening our leg while supporting and complementing the essential roles of family and church. Together, we provide the stable foundation young men need to grow into the leaders, husbands, fathers, and warriors God has called them to be.

---

5. *How do the roles of home, church, and Iron Academy complement each other in shaping a young man's identity and purpose?*

6. *What challenges might arise if one of these components is neglected or removed, and how can families and churches work together to ensure a stable foundation for their sons?*

Academic learning within community should also be joyful, though it demands effort. Targeted Learning aligns with young men's curiosity and developmental stages, guiding them through mastery, connection, and advanced thinking.

They start with foundational knowledge—answering the who, what, when, where, and why of a unit—ensuring a solid base. Exercises like summarizing, classifying, and cooperative learning then help them connect ideas, solidifying understanding and relevance. As knowledge deepens, they apply it through pattern recognition, comparative analysis, and hypothesis generation. This progression strengthens critical thinking and prepares them to synthesize and evaluate ideas, fostering creativity and problem-solving skills valued today.

Authentic assessments, debates, and hands-on projects—like dissecting specimens, building cell models, or constructing trebuchets in Algebra Two to test accuracy and distance—engage them dynamically. Targeted Learning ensures they're not just engaged but developing essential skills, transforming inquisitive young men into confident, thoughtful leaders.

Shooting a longbow accurately mirrors Targeted Learning's systematic approach, building intellectual mastery step-by-step as God designed the brain to learn. Just as hitting the bullseye requires precise stance, grip, draw, and release, mastering a subject demands foundational knowledge, analytical skills, and critical thinking.

The Mongols, famed for longbow mastery, shot birds from horseback through disciplined practice, calculating trajectory, speed, and distance under changing conditions. Similarly, Targeted Learning guides young men incrementally, blending foundational knowledge with analytical and critical thinking. Rather than lingering in lower-level learning (e.g., fill-in-the-blanks), they progress through multiple levels in every unit, building subject-specific thinking skills. This makes learning meaningful, cultivating higher-order thinking that young men enjoy and the world needs from its leaders.

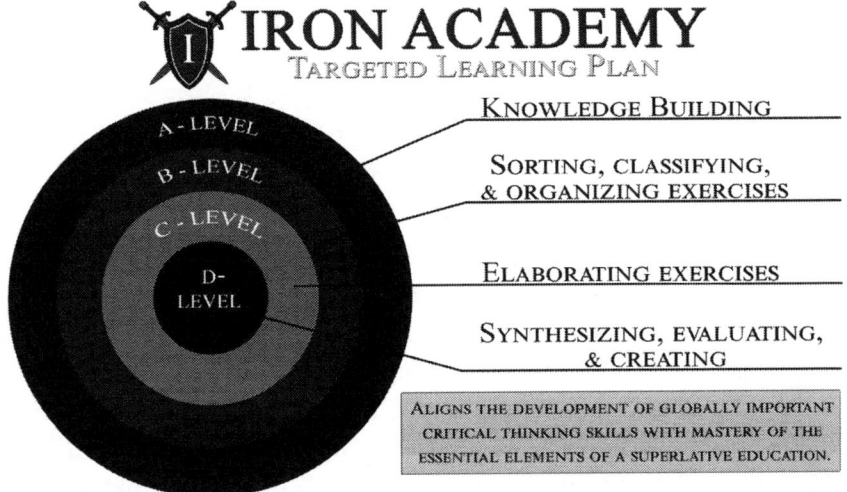

In eighth-grade U.S. History, studying the Antebellum Period isn't just memorizing dates. The target: craft a "Compromise of 1860" to avert the Civil War—something the U.S. Senate couldn't achieve. How? The teacher starts with the goal and works inward, like an archer aiming for the bullseye. A-Level learning covers the who, what, when, and where—events like the Missouri Compromise, Indian Removal Act, and Lincoln's "house divided" argument.

B- and C-Level thinking then challenges them further. Using retrieval practice and interleaving, students connect facts, analyze ideas, and retain knowledge durably summarizing events, classifying laws, or comparing compromises. C-Level analysis of the Lincoln-Douglas debates explores how slavery viewpoints shaped opinion, creating "desirable difficulties" for deeper comprehension.

At D-Level, equipped with a solid base and honed skills, they synthesize and evaluate, crafting their Compromise of 1860. Through Socratic discussions or presentations, they hypothesize, justify, and defend solutions. Like Mongol archers, they use precision and practice to achieve mastery. Targeted Learning taps their desire for purposeful work, making them eager to apply learning impactfully, preparing them to tackle real-world challenges with confidence and creativity.

Targeted Learning encourages grappling with history's beauty, unlike iPad- or Chromebook-based quizzing that often settles for regurgitated facts and low-level thinking. Which would you rather have done in middle school? Which learner would you hire? Targeted Learning engages, equips deep thinking, and yields greater long-term mastery.

Finally, young men experience greater joy and better outcomes—academically, physically, socially, immunologically, and emotionally—when physically active throughout the day. Movement benefits body, mind, and emotions. At Iron Academy, physical engagement extends beyond sports to outdoor adventures, team competitions, and frequent play.

Research in Pediatrics shows daily movement improves cognitive performance, focus, and memory, boosting academic outcomes. Activities like sports and challenges promote fitness, camaraderie, and teamwork, teaching perseverance, collaboration, and discipline—skills valuable in and out of class.

Frequent movement counters sedentary digital culture's harms. CDC data show sixty minutes of moderate-to-vigorous activity daily reduces depression, anxiety, and obesity. Iron Academy's Brain Breaks—brief movement opportunities—improve focus, reduce stress, and increase engagement. Daily physical education fosters a lifelong appreciation for fitness and health.

Physical activity also boosts immunity and long-term health. The *Journal of Adolescent Health* notes it enhances circulation, reduces inflammation, and supports disease resistance, lowering chronic illness risks. By integrating structured movement, Iron Academy builds habits for lifelong well-being.

Physical activity isn't just about fitness—it fosters holistic growth. Young men thrive finding joy in movement, teamwork, and overcoming challenges, preparing them to excel academically, maintain health, and build relationships, honoring the God who created them for purpose.

The Working Community is a dynamic workshop transforming young men through effort, resilience, and shared purpose. Embracing responsibility, collaborating with peers, and engaging in purposeful activities develop virtues for godly leadership and service.

This community refines the physical, emotional, and spiritual dimensions of manhood. Through responsibilities, accountability, unplugged learning, and physical engagement, young men discover the joy of purposeful living. They learn their work has value, their choices matter, and their character shapes the world.

Iron Academy equips young men not just to meet life's demands but to thrive within them, cultivating leaders ready to serve with diligence, humility, and strength. Here, resilience and responsibility take root, growing into lives of integrity and Christ-centered purpose—the foundation of Iron men, a legacy extending beyond these walls.

7. *Why is it important for young men to experience intellectual challenges that regularly require them to analyze, synthesize, and hypothesize, rather than simply recall facts?*

8. *How does Targeted Learning create a more meaningful academic experience for them?*

CHAPTER 7

THE FORGE OF JOY AND PURPOSE

Iron Academy's joyful and working community is an active forge, shaping young men into Christ-centered leaders ready for life's battles. Through brotherhood and discipleship, they experience the joy of accountability and purpose. Through challenges demanding resilience and responsibility, they find satisfaction in aligning with God's design.

This dual framework equips them to thrive in family, church, and community while preparing them to stand firm in cultural and spiritual fights. It instills virtues and strength to defend integrity and lead with courage and humility in a world craving godly examples.

Iron Academy doesn't just teach manhood—it calls young men to fight for it. The Keeper system, Accountability Days, and Honor Code are training grounds for warriors who'll uphold truth and grace in a fractured world.

The fight continues. As the next chapter reveals, "The Fight Culture" calls every teacher, parent, student, and stakeholder to pursue holiness, leadership, and excellence unwaveringly. This isn't just a community—it's a movement. The time to engage is now.

---

9. *In what ways does the combination of meaningful work and a joyful community at Iron Academy help students thrive both academically and personally?*

10. *How might schools that focus solely on academic results, without incorporating joy and meaningful work, fall short in preparing young people for the challenges of life beyond the classroom?*

RADICALLY COUNTER-CULTURAL:

THE SCHOOL THAT FIGHTS

Nehemiah 4:14 (ESV): "Remember the Lord, who is great and awesome, and fight for your brothers, your sons, your daughters, your wives, and your homes."

The Fight Culture at Iron Academy is a radical, countercultural response to a world that seeks to weaken, confuse, and undermine biblical manhood. This isn't a fight against people—it's a fight for young men, families, and the Kingdom of God. It's about standing firm, embracing responsibility, and training young men to reject passivity and lead with wisdom, strength, and love.

In a culture that isolates boys and discourages godly fatherhood, Iron Academy fights to restore what's been lost—God's design for building men. We fight for families, partnering with parents raising sons against a tide pulling them from truth. We fight for young men, equipping them with training, discipline, education, and discipleship to become faithful husbands, fathers, productive citizens, and leaders. We fight for the Kingdom, knowing godly men are vital to strong families, vibrant churches, and thriving communities.

This isn't a call to toxic aggression or domination. It's a call to conviction, perseverance, and faithfulness. "Fight" evokes struggle—an unrelenting pursuit of holiness, excellence, and shepherd-leadership. J.C. Ryle captured this well: "He who would understand the nature of true holiness must know that the Christian is 'a man of war.' If we would be holy—we must fight!" This echoes **Joshua 24:15: "Choose this day whom you will serve... But as for me and my house, we will serve the Lord."**

At Iron Academy, we reject the notion that manhood happens by chance. Boys don't become men through passivity, and holiness isn't inherited—it's fought for. God's people must choose this fight. Some fight alone, but Scripture shows we're stronger together, seeking wise counsel. The Fight Culture trains young men to stand firm, equips families to resist cultural passivity, and forges a brotherhood committed to truth and righteousness.

This fight isn't ours alone—it's a battle waged by God's people across generations. Its biblical foundation resounds throughout Scripture, calling us to stand, resist, and fight for righteousness.

8th Grade Unplugged:

The eighth grade is often the low point of a young man's life—a hormonal rollercoaster of contradictions. These young men are simultaneously full of hubris and have no self-confidence. They are changing hormonally, physically, emotionally, and socially. They push away Mom. They push away Dad. They find faults in their formerly heroic teachers. They are keenly interested in female body parts. They question their faith. It's a perfect storm of confusion and mood swings.

All of this is natural, but all of this can be done in a way that either honors God or dishonors God and everyone else. The world is telling them to dishonor everything. The world wants them to tear one another down, to denigrate their parents, to talk about girls' bodies, and to unite in the unshakable certainty that the entire world hates them. If it didn't so often cause so much pain, it would be comical—but this gloriously awkward battlefield where confidence and cluelessness wage daily war makes families wonder how they could have failed so miserably.

I encourage every family, "This is all natural and somehow part of God's developmental plan. You probably went through or witnessed similar things when you were in eighth grade. Let's keep working together. He is not who he is going to be yet. He will come back. Seriously, don't forget that he is not who he is going to be yet."

So, what do we do differently? We spend more time with eighth graders than anyone else. We decided many years ago that we could either suffer through every school's recurring nightmare or do something about it. We started 8th Grade Unplugged, the Keeper program, and regular check-ins throughout the year. It has made all the difference.

Every October, we take a week off for Unplugged to enjoy the fall weather and camp out at the lake. We usually have hundreds of lakeside acres all to ourselves. We invite the dads, make lots of global-warming-inducing-sized fires, cook our own food over the flames or with our multiple Blackstone griddles, read our Bibles, learn how to pray through Psalm 23 for transformation as God's shepherd leaders, talk about everything, have tons of fun, fish, swim in the cold October water, freely explore the hundreds of acres surrounding us, play football and spike ball on the sandy beach, and every night wrestle with who we should be and want to be.

We talk about how they're treating one another and how they're treating their moms. The unspoken tensions bubble up around the campfire, and sometimes for the first time, they deal with them. They come up with the changes they want to make in themselves. They keep one another accountable. We keep them accountable. They bond like never before. By the time we pack up, these young men have changed or have begun to embrace that they must change. They stand taller, speak with more confidence, and—miraculously—treat their moms with newfound respect...because they know Coach Mitchell, Mr. Anderson, and I are going to ask them frequently in the carline in the mornings!

THE BIBLICAL FOUNDATION OF THE FIGHT CULTURE

"Fight Culture" isn't a biblical phrase, but its call to spiritual battle, perseverance, and holiness weaves through Scripture. From Genesis to Revelation, God's people are summoned to stand firm, resist evil, and fight for righteousness. Godliness isn't passive—it's pursued.

In Exodus 15:3: *"The Lord is a man of war; the Lord is his name,"* God is a warrior. This isn't just imagery—it's reality.

Joshua 1:9 commands: *"Be strong and courageous... for the Lord your God is with you wherever you go."* Strength and courage aren't optional—they're essential for advancing God's Kingdom.

Nehemiah 4:14 intensifies this: *"Remember the Lord... and fight for your brothers, your sons, your daughters, your wives, and your homes."* The battle is generational, defending family, faith, and truth.

The New Testament shifts to spiritual warfare. Ephesians 6:10-18 urges believers to *"put on the full armor of God"* against cosmic powers.

Paul reflects in 2 Timothy 4:7: *"I have fought the good fight, I have finished the race, I have kept the faith."* Faith is a struggle—a war to be won.

THE FIGHT CULTURE AT IRON ACADEMY

At Iron Academy, this biblical mandate defines The Fight Culture. It is not a passive philosophy but an active response to the reality of spiritual warfare. The Fight Culture demands that students, staff, and families reject passivity and actively engage in the pursuit of holiness, wisdom, and excellence.

Like the warriors of Scripture, students are called to *"put on the full armor of God"* (Ephesians 6:10–18), equipping themselves with truth, righteousness, and faith in preparation for the battles they will face. They are charged to be *"strong and courageous"* (Joshua 1:9) in their academic, social, and spiritual lives, standing firm against a culture that seeks to soften and sideline them. Families are summoned to *"fight for their sons and daughters"* (Nehemiah 4:14), raising them to be men who will defend their homes, churches, and communities with integrity and strength.

The Fight Culture is not for the faint of heart. Iron Academy students, staff, and families are flawed, fallen, and in constant need of grace. But they are warriors in training—learning to embrace hardship, persevere in the face of failure, and rise again stronger. This is a place where men are forged, not coddled; where excellence is demanded, not suggested; where brotherhood is built through accountability, not convenience.

This is a fight for holiness, for excellence, for unity, for students, and for the mission itself. It is a battle that requires intentionality, resilience, and unwavering commitment. It is an all-encompassing charge to reject mediocrity, embrace discomfort, and cultivate the discipline necessary to lead in faith and truth.

This battle does not belong to one group alone. It is not just for students or staff, nor is it confined to the walls of the academy. This fight extends beyond the classroom, beyond the home, beyond even the church—it calls for an entire movement. It demands an army—a community—an unyielding front committed to raising up a new generation of godly men.

Enter The Iron Front.

1. *What is your first reaction to "Iron Academy: The School That Fights!"*

2. *Many people are initially repulsed by the phrasing. How might a radically intentional follower of Jesus interpret "The School That Fights!" very differently than a casual Christian or an unbeliever?*

THE IRON FRONT: A CALL TO ARMS FOR THE COMMUNITY

While the language of "fighting" permeates our mission, Iron Academy is not a place of harsh discipline or joyless striving. It is a place of camaraderie, growth, brotherly love, joy, and deep fulfillment. The fight is not about rigid obedience—it is about standing shoulder to shoulder with brothers, sharpening one another, and discovering the joy of living fully as God-designed men. Iron Academy is a school filled with laughter, friendships forged in challenge—and a deep sense of belonging. We train with intensity not because we must, but because we love the mission and one another.

At Iron Academy, *The Fight Culture* is not a mere slogan—it is a declaration of purpose, a rallying cry, and a way of life. It represents our commitment to actively fighting for the biblical ideals of manhood in a world that offers no clear pathway to it. Modern culture does not naturally produce strong, godly men; it produces confusion, passivity, and complacency. You likely see this every day in your community. *The Fight Culture* stands in direct opposition to this tide, calling young men to embrace challenge, reject mediocrity, and pursue holiness, wisdom, and responsibility with relentless determination.

To fight for biblical manhood is to fight against passivity. It is to recognize that young men will not drift into strength, leadership, or spiritual maturity—they must be trained to it. We have a long-time mantra at Iron Academy that captures the sentiment: "Because biblical manhood is never an accident!" *The Fight Culture* at Iron Academy calls students to embrace the discomfort of growth, to take responsibility for themselves and their communities, and to step into their God-given roles as shepherd-leaders. They are taught to resist the ease of a soft, indulgent life and instead develop the grit, integrity, and conviction necessary to lead with strength and wisdom.

For the staff—male and female—at Iron Academy, *The Fight Culture* means living out their faith daily in front of students. For male staff members, it means modeling biblical manhood with authenticity, guiding young men not just through words but through example. It is similar for female staff members, but they need to live and interact with the young men in such a way that encourages them to biblical manhood. Staff members serve as allies to radically intentional Christian parents, standing shoulder to shoulder with them in the work of discipleship. They do not replace parents but reinforce their efforts, ensuring that Iron Academy remains a place where young men see a unified front in their formation—at home, in their church, and at school.

For Iron Parents, *The Fight Culture* is an invitation to actively participate in the process of forging their sons into strong, God-honoring men. It is a reminder that they are not alone in this battle—that Iron Academy fights alongside them, reinforcing the biblical principles they have upheld for years in their homes. It is also a challenge to remain steadfast in their calling as the people primarily responsible for discipling their children, to resist the cultural pressures that seek to soften or redefine biblical parenting.

For Iron Board Members, *The Fight Culture* is a commitment to safeguarding the mission of Iron Academy, ensuring that it remains unwaveringly faithful to its biblical foundations. It means prioritizing vision over comfort, making decisions that serve the long-term spiritual and leadership development of students rather than settling for the status quo. Board members are entrusted with the responsibility of ensuring that Iron Academy continues to be a training ground for godly young men, equipped to fight for truth, their families, and their faith in an increasingly hostile world.

Iron Stakeholders are the supply lines in the battle for biblical manhood, ensuring Iron Academy remains a training ground for godly leaders. *The Fight Culture* for Iron Stakeholders is not passive charity but active engagement in equipping young men to resist cultural passivity and compromise. Their investment provides the tools of rigorous academics, discipleship, and leadership training, forging men who will stand firm in their homes, churches, and communities. In a world that seeks to strip young men of purpose, Iron Stakeholders fight by sustaining a mission that builds warriors for truth.

The following sections will explore what *The Fight Culture* looks like for each of these groups—Iron Students, Iron Staff, Iron Parents, Iron Board Members, and Iron Stakeholders—demonstrating how this shared commitment to fighting for biblical manhood shapes every aspect of life at Iron Academy. This is not a passive journey. It is an active battle for the hearts, minds, and futures of young men. The world is not neutral; it is either forming them into strong, godly leaders or weakening them into passive, directionless men. At Iron Academy, we choose to fight. As for this Iron Community, we choose to serve the Lord. We choose to fight!

Iron Students

The Fight Culture at Iron Academy is more than just a concept—it's a way of life that shapes young men's identity, challenges their character, and equips them with the strength to stand firm in a world that constantly seeks to weaken and redefine biblical manhood. This culture calls students to reject passivity, embrace challenges, and actively pursue their God-given purpose. Students do not merely endure hardship; they revel in the joy of brotherhood, with halls filled with laughter, encouragement, and resilience. The "fight" is not one of suffering but of discovery—finding joy in overcoming obstacles, learning deeply, and building lifelong friendships with brothers who will stand beside them for years to come. They experience the thrill of hard work, the pride of mastering new skills, and the satisfaction of growing into the men they were meant to be. Iron Academy is not a monastery or battlefield; it is a family, united by a common purpose, bonded in shared struggle, and filled with contagious joy. The atmosphere is shockingly different from other schools, public or private. Iron Academy is welcoming, energetic, and joyful.

For Iron Academy students, *The Fight Culture* is a daily commitment to growth, where drifting through the school years is not an option. From the moment they step off the bus at Crucible Camp; they are confronted with high expectations. Challenged to fight against mediocrity, passivity, and apathy, every day calls them to push themselves further—academically, spiritually, and personally. They are expected to embrace discipline, self-mastery, and excellence in all areas of life. Whether in the classroom, on the athletic field, or in their personal interactions, they learn that nothing worthwhile is achieved without intentional effort and perseverance. As Mr. Anderson has taught, "Intentionality has its own rewards."

Students understand that they are not passive consumers of education, but active participants in their development. In every challenge they face, they learn that growth requires effort and perseverance. *The Fight Culture* is not just about personal development; it is about preparing young men to step into their calling as Christlike leaders. The world does not need more young men waiting for permission to lead; it needs those trained to lead with humility, courage, love, and conviction. Leadership is not about titles or awards; it's a daily responsibility. Every student is placed in leadership roles—through student governance, mentoring younger peers, or leading discussions. They are given opportunities to make real decisions, take responsibility for outcomes, and learn from their mistakes. Leadership is about serving others and stewarding influence for God's glory. *The Fight Culture* instills in young men a deep sense of purpose—to live as shepherd-leaders who will one day lead their families, churches, and communities with wisdom and integrity.

Iron Academy's *Fight Culture* also calls students to reject passivity and weakness, confronting the temptation to retreat into self-indulgence. Young men are trained to resist the easy path and embrace a life of purpose and action. They are taught to reject the lie that following Jesus is automatic, to fight against mediocrity, and to abandon victimhood. They learn to take ownership and responsibility, resisting the apathy that encourages standing for nothing. Students are not coddled or protected from life's difficulties—they are equipped to face challenges head-on.

Opportunities to wrestle with tough questions, experience failure, and develop resilience are essential parts of their training for manhood.

A core element of *The Fight Culture* is preparing young men for the responsibilities of future marriage, fatherhood, and church leadership. Many young men today enter adulthood unprepared for these challenges, and Iron Academy sees this as a crisis worth fighting against. Students are taught that biblical manhood is about sacrificial leadership, brotherly love, and unwavering commitment, not domination or entitlement. They are trained to take responsibility for their actions, develop habits of discipline and integrity, and prepare to lead their families with wisdom, strength, and faithfulness.

Physical and spiritual strength are core to *The Fight Culture*, with students encouraged to develop both. Physical training teaches discipline, endurance, and perseverance—lessons that translate into all areas of life. Spiritual training equips them to fight against sin, temptation, and the lies of the world with biblical truth. Iron Academy's Fight Culture aims to produce young men who are not fragile or easily swayed by cultural trends, but men of conviction, grit, and enduring faith.

For students, *The Fight Culture* means being part of something greater than themselves—preparing not just for college or a career, but for a life of impact, leadership, and faithfulness. They are part of a brotherhood that will challenge them, an education that will sharpen them, and a mission that will define them. Life at Iron Academy is about fighting for what matters: truth, family, and the King. It is the school that fights, and students are trained to become the warriors the world desperately needs.

Ask any Iron graduate and they won't share stories of suffering— they'll talk about brotherhood, life-changing experiences, and friendships that have carried them into adulthood. They'll recall moments of victory after challenges, of teachers who invested in them, and the exhilarating realization that they are ready to lead. Iron Academy is not about producing hardened soldiers; it's about forming joyful warriors—men who step into the world with confidence, faith, and the deep satisfaction of knowing they are fully equipped for the road ahead.

IRON STAFF

The Fight Culture is not only something that shapes the students at Iron Academy—it is a way of life that must be embraced by those who lead and train them. The staff members at Iron Academy are not merely educators; they are mentors, warriors, and standard-bearers in the battle for biblical manhood. Their role is not just to teach subjects but to model resilience, discipline, and Christlike leadership in a world that desperately needs strong, godly men.

Just as students are expected to reject passivity and embrace discomfort, so too must the staff. They stand on the front lines, walking alongside students as they grow in faith, wisdom, and strength, demonstrating daily what it means to fight for holiness, truth, and excellence.

At Iron Academy, staff members are not just educators—they are warriors in the fight for biblical manhood. Every teacher, administrator, and coach steps into this role with the understanding that their work goes far beyond delivering lessons or managing classrooms. Their mission is to forge young men into leaders who will stand firm in a world that seeks to soften and undermine biblical masculinity. To do this effectively, staff members must live out *The Fight Culture* themselves, modeling resilience, wisdom, and conviction in all they do.

This means that Iron Academy staff do not simply talk about high expectations—they uphold them in their own lives. They reject the complacency that plagues modern education, where teachers are often more concerned with convenience than excellence. Instead, they embrace the challenge of pushing students beyond what they think they are capable of, demanding their best efforts in academics, leadership, and personal character.

Staff members at Iron Academy do not simply assign work–they engage with students, challenge their thinking, and hold them accountable to the highest standards of integrity and discipline.

But their role extends beyond academics. Staff members are also spiritual mentors, shepherding students as they navigate the pressures and temptations of adolescence. They do not shrink back from difficult conversations or avoid addressing the tough issues young men face today. Instead, they lean in. They call students to holiness, guiding them through their struggles, and reminding them that the battle for biblical manhood is fought not just with intellect and discipline, but with faith, prayer, and dependence on Christ.

Their influence is not confined to the classroom; it extends to daily discipleship groups, chores, Accountability Days, teams, extracurricular clubs, and daily interactions where they encourage, correct, and disciple the young men entrusted to their care.

This level of investment requires staff members to reject the modern notion of teaching as a detached profession. They are not merely disseminators of information—they are builders of men.

This means their own lives must be marked by the same pursuit of holiness and excellence they expect from students. They must be men and women of prayer, wisdom, and unwavering conviction. They must be prepared to challenge cultural lies, stand firm on biblical truth, encourage, build young men, and demonstrate the kind of leadership that students can emulate.

Showing Up/Funerals:

One of the clearest signs of love and respect is presence. And yet, I've noticed that younger people often choose not to show up for life's hardest moments, especially funerals. Maybe it's discomfort. Maybe it's busyness.

Maybe it's the feeling that their presence won't change anything. But love—especially brotherly love—calls us to something greater. It calls us to stand beside one another, not just in celebration but also in sorrow. True love is not about convenience. It is about commitment.

At Iron Academy, we refuse to let this lesson be lost. From the very beginning, we made a commitment: we show up. If a student or staff member loses a loved one and the funeral is within driving distance, we are there. Whether it's for a former student, Johnny's grandfather, or Mr. Parker's dad, Iron Academy students stand alongside those who grieve, not as mere acquaintances but as brothers.

It may seem like a small thing, but I don't believe it is. In moments of deep loss, words often fail, but love does not. Presence speaks volumes. Few things say "You matter to me" more than showing up when you don't have to—when you choose to bear another's burden simply because they are your brother.

IRON PARENTS

Just as the staff at Iron Academy embrace *The Fight Culture* by modeling Christlike leadership and mentorship, so too must the parents who send their sons to be forged in this environment. Iron Academy does not replace the role of parents. It partners with them in the sacred task of raising godly young men.

The Fight Culture cannot be confined to the walls of the school. It must be reinforced in the home. Iron Parents are not passive observers; they must be the most active participants in the fight for their sons' spiritual, intellectual, and moral formation.

Their previous, current, and ongoing willingness to stand firm, uphold high expectations, and disciple their sons daily is what allows *The Fight Culture* to take deep root and bear lasting fruit.

Parents who choose Iron Academy are not looking for a school that simply prepares their sons for college and career; they are seeking an institution that will fight alongside them to shape their sons into men of courage, wisdom, and faith. *The Fight Culture* is not just about what happens during the school day—it is a partnership between home, school, and church that requires parents to be fully engaged in their sons' formation. Iron Parents want a school that will fight for them and for their son.

Iron Parents are those who are willing to make the hard choices. They understand that raising a son in today's world requires intentionality and vigilance. They reject the passive approach to parenting that allows culture to dictate the values their sons absorb. Instead, they fight for their sons' purity, their discipline, their faith, and their ability to think critically. They set boundaries that align with biblical wisdom, limiting the influence of technology and distractions that threaten to undermine their son's development. They do not simply hope their son will become a godly man. They work diligently, in partnership with their local church and Iron Academy, to ensure it.

A core aspect of *The Fight Culture* for parents is their active involvement in their sons' lives. They are not disengaged, leaving the work of discipleship to the school or the church. If parents aren't doing it at home, we can't win. We won't try. Iron Parents pray with their sons, engage in deep conversations, and model godly character in their own lives. They set an example of faithfulness by prioritizing church attendance, serving their communities, and upholding biblical convictions in their households. Their sons see in them a living example of what it means to be a man or woman who fights for the things that matter.

IRON DADS

For fathers, this means stepping fully into their role as shepherds of their homes. *The Fight Culture* demands that fathers be more than providers—they must be spiritual leaders, guiding their sons in truth, discipline, and love. They must be present, engaged, and willing to have the difficult conversations that shape young men's character.

At Iron Academy, young men do not simply hear about biblical manhood—they see it lived out in the lives of their fathers, staff members, and mentors. The alignment between school and home is critical, and when a father embraces The Fight Culture, his son is far more likely to do the same.

Many of our fathers are highly engaged in our Fight Club for Dads, a powerful program to equip fathers to engage successfully in their fight to fulfill their calling within their homes.

Fight Club for Dads:

The idea for a "Fight Club" for fathers began one morning with a conversation with a very intentional Iron Dad. He wanted to discuss his son's worthiness to receive a marker of accomplishment toward earning his Challenge Coin. This father, a first-generation follower of Jesus, was concerned that he might be at least a partial hindrance to his son's progression in the pursuit of true biblical manhood–not because he wanted to be an obstacle, mind you, but since he wasn't raised in a Christian home, he felt that he wasn't fully prepared to come alongside his own sons in their growing desire for Christ-like holiness. In other words, dad felt like he might be the "weak link" in the chain...he just wasn't sure. This uncertainty drove him to inquire about the possibility of creating some kind of fellowship opportunity with other dads who had similar unvoiced concerns, or those more experienced fathers who felt that they could offer some advice to those men in quiet need. And with that articulated thought, Fight Club for dads was born. We meet once or twice a month to share our battles as husbands, fathers, and biblical men—living in a world overtly hostile to Christ-centered manhood. Furthermore, sons who also wish to attend, are welcomed, so that they might learn that the fight for holiness, as J.C. Ryle called it, is best fought with other intentional Christian men who are in this great war as well.

(Rich Anderson, Iron Principal)

Iron Moms

Mothers always play an essential role in this fight. The world is waging war on their sons, seeking to pull them away from biblical truth and into confusion and weakness. Mothers who embrace *The Fight Culture* do not give in to fear; they stand firm. They recognize that raising a strong, godly son in today's world requires them to be both nurturing and unwavering. They encourage their sons to embrace challenge, to step into responsibility, and to fight for what is right. They do not shield their sons from discomfort but instead help them navigate it with wisdom and faith. They trust Iron Academy to push their sons beyond what is easy because they know that true manhood is forged through struggle and perseverance.

An Iron Mom's Thoughts

As a Christian mother of sons, my greatest desire is for them to mature into strong, God-honoring men—leaders of integrity who will guide their families with wisdom and faith. I want them to understand the value of diligence and hard work, embrace respect and responsibility, and cultivate meaningful, God-centered relationships. We are so grateful for the added blessing of finding a school that shares these same values and partners with us every day.

We are seven years into our journey at Iron Academy, and I can confidently say that this school is not just our sons' place of learning— it is like a family. It serves as a support system as we teach and guide our sons toward Jesus. As a mom, I envisioned a school for our sons that felt like a true community—where teachers are more than educators; they are mentors, role models, and trusted allies. I dreamed of teachers who would genuinely invest in our sons, championing their growth and development as passionately as we do. A school that knows exactly who our sons are and provides honest, encouraging, and constructive feedback, all with the goal of nurturing their growth through the lens of faith.

We wanted an education that would challenge our sons to think critically, work diligently, and take pride in their efforts—all while fostering strong relationships and lifelong friendships. Most importantly, we sought a school that would partner with us in reinforcing the same values we teach at home. One might think such a school is impossible to find—yet we feel profoundly grateful to have found Iron Academy. It has exceeded our expectations.

Our oldest son is a senior this year. Throughout his time at IA, he has grown in confidence, leadership, maturity, and faith. He stands firmly on God's Word, embracing what it means to be a biblical son, brother, and, one day, a husband and father. Our hearts are filled with gratitude for the unwavering partnership we've shared with Iron Academy over the years. It is a true blessing to know that this school has played such a vital role in shaping our sons into the men God has called them to be.

(Sarah Watkins, Iron Super Mom)

One might think we only serve perfect nuclear families. However, to date, we have yet to encounter a perfect family, and single moms often "get" biblical manhood better than anyone. They deeply understand the pain that accompanies the absence of godly manhood! No, we serve homes that actively pursue Jesus—warts and all.

Iron Parents do not walk this journey alone. They are part of a community—a tribe of like-minded families, all of whom are committed to the same mission. They support, pray for, and challenge one another to remain steadfast. The relationships formed among Iron Families strengthen the entire school community, creating a network of encouragement and accountability that extends beyond the classroom and into every aspect of life.

Ultimately, *The Fight Culture* means that parents recognize the stakes. They understand that the world is not neutral in shaping their sons; it is actively working against them. But rather than surrendering to the culture, Iron Parents stand firm. They fight for their sons' hearts, minds, and futures, ensuring that they are equipped to become godly men who will lead their own families, churches, and communities with conviction and faithfulness.

The Fight Culture does not end at graduation. It is a lifelong commitment, one that parents, staff, and students embrace together. The world needs men who will stand firm, who will reject passivity, and who will lead with strength and wisdom. Iron Academy is committed to forging such men, but it can only do so in partnership with families who are willing to fight for the same vision.

IRON BOARD MEMBERS

Just as Iron Academy depends on dedicated parents to reinforce *The Fight Culture* in the home and committed staff to model it on campus, it also relies on strong, mission-driven leadership at the highest level to ensure the school remains true to its calling for generations to come. This responsibility falls to the Iron Academy Board of Directors, a governing body tasked with protecting the school's mission, vision, and long-term effectiveness.

The Fight Culture is not only for students being forged into godly leaders or for the parents and staff who disciple them. It also extends to those who oversee and safeguard the institution itself. Iron Board Members are more than decision-makers; they are guardians of the mission, stewards of the vision, and warriors who stand firm against mission drift, compromise, and mediocrity.

The Iron Board does not exist to micromanage daily operations; it exists to set the strategic direction, ensure organizational health, and hold leadership accountable to the mission. As a governance-run school, the board is responsible for hiring, developing, and, if necessary, removing the CEO. They establish high-level objectives that align with the school's mission, ensuring that Iron Academy remains unwavering in its commitment to forging young men into godly leaders, deep thinkers, resilient disciples, and bold warriors. Their role is one of protection, oversight, and long-term stewardship.

Iron Board Members fight for the school by safeguarding its vision from compromise. The pressures of modern education, cultural shifts, and even well-intentioned but misguided influences can slowly erode an institution's founding principles. Iron Academy's board exists to resist these forces, maintaining the school's biblical foundation and ensuring that it never deviates from its calling. They protect against mission drift by staying rooted in Iron Academy's original intent: to forge young men for Christ and equip them for leadership in their families, churches, and communities.

In alignment with *The Fight Culture*, Iron Board Members do not simply attend meetings and review budgets—they engage in the battle for biblical manhood by ensuring that the school remains a place where young men are taught truth, challenged to grow, and equipped to lead. They oversee the financial health of the institution, ensuring that resources are allocated wisely and that the school remains sustainable for future generations. They champion the school's vision in their communities, connecting with donors, churches, and like-minded families who share the commitment to raising godly men.

The accountability that *The Fight Culture* demands of students is equally expected of board members. Just as students are held to high standards, board members hold themselves and the school's leadership accountable to the highest level of integrity, wisdom, and excellence. Their decisions are not based on what is easiest, most popular, or financially expedient; they are made through the lens of the Bible and Iron Academy's mission. Every policy, financial decision, and strategic initiative is measured against one key question: Does this decision strengthen Iron Academy's ability to forge men who will fight for Christ?

---

3. *The Iron Academy Mission Statement reads: "Iron Academy exists to glorify God by training young men to be unwavering in faith, adept in leadership, and growing in His wisdom; equipping them to fight for biblical values, strengthen their families, and serve as leaders in their churches and communities." It can be quite difficult to capture an organization's mission statement succinctly. What would you change about it? What does it get right? What would be better?*

Iron Board Members also serve as protectors of the leadership culture within the school. They invest in the development of the CEO, ensuring that the person leading Iron Academy is fully aligned with *The Fight Culture*. They provide mentorship, oversight, and strategic guidance, ensuring that the CEO has the support and accountability needed to execute the vision effectively. This relationship is one of mutual commitment—just as the board expects the CEO to lead with conviction, the CEO expects the board to remain steadfast in its role as the governing authority of the school.

> 4. *The Iron Academy's Vision Statement reads, "To build an unshakeable brotherhood of warriors for Christ who fight boldly for truth and righteousness, leading their families, strengthening their churches, and serving their communities with wisdom, courage, honor, and love." We want it to present a clear picture of the future it seeks to build in alignment with biblical values and mission. What do you envision when you hear, "an unshakeable brotherhood of warriors for Christ?"*

Perhaps most importantly, Iron Board Members fight for the future. They recognize that the battle for biblical manhood is generational. The decisions they make today impact not only the students currently enrolled but the generations of young men who will one day walk through Iron Academy's doors. They do not merely think about the present—they plan for the long-term sustainability and expansion of the mission. Whether it is securing funding for capital campaigns, expanding opportunities for students, or strengthening partnerships with churches and donors, board members are continually working to ensure that Iron Academy remains a beacon of light for generations to come.

The Fight Culture is not just a philosophy for students—it is the guiding principle for every level of Iron Academy's leadership. The board exists to ensure that this culture remains intact, that the mission is never diluted, and that the vision continues to grow. They fight for Iron Academy with wisdom, prayer, and strategic action–knowing that their stewardship of this institution plays a crucial role in shaping the next generation of godly men.

THE IRON CHURCHES

Just as Iron Academy depends on a committed board to safeguard its mission, it also relies on strong, Bible-believing churches that actively call fathers and sons to reject passivity and lead with conviction. *The Fight Culture* is not isolated—it thrives within churches that boldly preach truth, disciple families, and equip young men to embrace godly responsibility. Whether or not they know of Iron Academy, these churches are already engaged in the same battle, forging men who will lead their families and advance the Kingdom.

Iron Churches build Iron Academy families, shaping them long before they apply and strengthening them as they raise their sons with biblical conviction. These churches do not shrink from the fight; they call fathers to shepherd their homes and train young men for leadership.

Iron Academy does not stand apart from them—it stands with them, forging young men to return as leaders in their congregations. *The Fight Culture* begins in churches that refuse to surrender to cultural decay, raising up families who are already preparing their sons to be warriors for Christ.

CONCLUSION

Iron Academy is not merely a school—it is a mission field, a training ground, and a community united in the sacred work of forging godly men. *The Fight Culture* binds together students, staff, parents, board members, and churches in a shared mission that transcends education to become a way of life—a life of purpose, conviction, and unyielding resolve.

We are the school that fights! This fight is not easy, and we do not pretend otherwise. The world does not drift toward righteousness; it slides relentlessly into compromise. Popular culture does not raise strong, godly men; it weakens them with confusion, passivity, and distraction. The mission of Iron Academy is urgent because the stakes are eternal. We do not retreat. We do not compromise. We do not waver. We fight! We fight for our students to become the men God has called them to be—men of courage, wisdom, and faith. We fight for families who refuse to let the culture define their sons. We fight for staff and board members who carry the banner of biblical excellence with unrelenting determination. We fight for churches that boldly proclaim truth and disciple men to live it out. We fight because the next generation of men—their future families, their churches, their communities—depends on what we do right now.

As united members of the Iron Academy community, we do not settle for just educating. We do not stop at discipling. We build men—men who will stand firm, lead boldly, and live faithfully. And we fight for them every single day.

Iron Academy is not merely a school that fights—it is a school that builds men who find deep joy in the journey. Our graduates do not leave merely prepared; they leave filled—filled with the joy of brotherhood forged in shared struggle, the thrill of conquering challenges alongside their Iron brothers, and the deep satisfaction of knowing they are fully equipped for the next stage of life. This fight is not a burden—it is a gift, a privilege, a calling. It forges young men into leaders, friends, husbands, and fathers who will stand unwavering in both faith and joy for generations to come.

THE FIGHT BEGINS HERE: A CLOSING CALL TO ACTION

"The Christian life is very much like climbing a hill of ice. You cannot slide up. You have to cut every step with an ice axe. Only with incessant labor in cutting and chipping can you make any progress. If you want to know how to backslide, leave off going forward. Cease going upward, and you will go downward by necessity."

(Charles Spurgeon)

The battle for biblical manhood is raging, and the culture is not waiting. It is shaping the next generation—whether we engage or not. But we refuse to be passive. We refuse to surrender ground. We choose to fight. *The Fight Culture* is not just a philosophy; it is a call to arms—a summons to every heart stirred by these words. Every reader of this book now stands at a crossroads. Will you step into the fight? Will you join the ranks of those who refuse to let this generation be lost to passivity, confusion, and compromise?

If you are a **parent or grandparent,** your son or grandson is already in the battle. The only question is whether he is equipped to win it. Do not wait. The world will not wait. Schedule a tour of Iron Academy today and see firsthand how young men are being forged into leaders, warriors, and men of conviction. Let him step into an environment that challenges him, sharpens him, and prepares him to stand firm in the calling God has placed on his life. Choose a school that fights for you, for him, and for Him!

> **"To each, there comes in their lifetime a special moment when they are figuratively tapped on the shoulder and invited to do something unique to their talents. What a tragedy if that moment finds them unprepared or unwilling."**

(Winston Churchill)

If you are a **donor,** you are the supply line in this battle. The enemy is well-funded, and we must be too. Your investment is not charity—it is weaponry for a war worth fighting. You were created for just such a time as this. If you seek joy in your generosity, join the Fight Campaign—not as a faceless contributor, but as an essential warrior in the fight to reclaim God's design for men and advance His kingdom right here, right now.

If you **see the need for Iron Academy in your own city,** step forward. The time for hoping, waiting, or wondering if someone else will act is over. If God is stirring your heart, He is calling you to action. Register at ironacademy.org to receive information about bringing *The Fight Culture* to your community. Fuel the initiative to equip and mobilize leaders to launch new Iron Academies across the nation. Help us establish outposts in this movement for Christ-centered, battle-ready education.

This is not a passive call. This is an active enlistment. The world does not need more spectators—it needs warriors. The next generation of men—their future families, churches, and communities—depends on what God's men and women do today. The war for biblical manhood has already begun. The only question that remains is:

Will you fight?

THE FIGHT CLUB: TRAINING BROTHERHOOD FOR CHRIST

As more families, churches, and communities recognize the urgent need to fight for biblical manhood, many have asked for practical tools to engage in this battle. The Fight Club curriculum was developed in response to this growing need—offering structured, biblically-based programs to equip men, young men, and families with the training they need to stand firm in today's culture.

Each Fight Club curriculum—whether for dads, middle school, high school, young Adults, or families—provides 12 to 15 weeks of intensive discipleship designed to build a brotherhood for Christ. These are not merely discussion groups; they are training grounds where participants learn to reject passivity, embrace responsibility, and live with purpose and conviction.

> **"It is not the critic who counts; not the man who points out how the strong man stumbles... The credit belongs to the man who is actually in the arena, whose face is marred by dust and sweat and blood... who errs, who comes short again and again... but who does actually strive to do the deeds... who knows great enthusiasms,**

the great devotions; who spends himself in a worthy cause..."

(Theodore Roosevelt, The Man in the Arena, 1910)

Fight Club for Dads meets fathers where they are in their spiritual journey, offering wisdom from seasoned fathers alongside biblical teaching on leading their families with strength and humility. Fight Club for middle school and high school creates a brotherhood of young men who encourage one another to stand firm in their faith and embrace God's design for biblical manhood. Fight Club for Families brings the entire family unit together to establish Christ-centered patterns and build a legacy of faith.

These resources are available to churches and individuals who share our commitment to raising godly men. For more information on bringing Fight Club to your church or community, or to order materials for your family, visit ironacademy.org/fightclub. For a complete overview of all Fight Club resources, see Fight Club Bonus Content.

HONOR CODE CATEGORIES, VIRTUES, *and* DISPOSITIONS

HONOR CODE CATEGORY	VIRTUE	DEFINITION	BIBLE VERSES	DISPOSITION
Gentleman	Wisdom & Prudence	Exercising wisdom.	Proverbs 8:12, James 1:5, Proverbs 3:13–18	Thoughtfulness and careful consideration
Gentleman	Civility	Actively devising good for others and submitting your will for that of others; never disparaging or being unkind to a person for God-given attributes.	Philippians 2:3–4, Romans 12:10, 1 Corinthians 10:24	Respectfulness and empathy
Gentleman	Patience	Enduring trials and difficulties with steadfastness and trust in God's timing.	Romans 5:3–4, James 1:2–4, Galatians 6:9	Calmness and tolerance

HONOR CODE CATEGORY	VIRTUE	DEFINITION	BIBLE VERSES	DISPOSITION
Gentleman	Courage	Acting boldly and fearlessly in accordance with one's faith and convictions, even in the face of challenges, adversity, or danger.	Joshua 1:9, 2 Timothy 1:7, Psalm 27:14	Boldness and confidence in faith
Gentleman	Gentleness	Treating others with kindness and consideration.	Philippians 4:5, Colossians 3:12, Titus 3:2	Kindness and compassion
Gentleman	Self-Control	Exercising discipline over one's desires and impulses.	Galatians 5:22-23, 2 Timothy 1:7, 1 Corinthians 9:25	Discipline and mindfulness

HONOR CODE CATEGORY	VIRTUE	DEFINITION	BIBLE VERSES	DISPOSITION
Gentleman	Perseverance & Diligence	Persistent and careful effort in all aspects of life, guided by a commitment to honor God, fulfill responsibilities, and pursue excellence.	Colossians 3:23, Proverbs 10:4, 2 Thessalonians 3:10	Persistence and reliability
Gentleman	Reject Passivity	Be proactive, engaged, and purposeful—avoid inactivity and passivity in life, leadership, and faith.	Ephesians 5:15-16, Colossians 4:5, 1 Peter 5:8	Proactivity and engagement
Live Pure	Temperance	Exercising moderation, self-control, and avoiding excess or extremes.	Philippians 4:5, 1 Corinthians 9:25, Titus 2:12	Balance and restraint

HONOR CODE CATEGORY	VIRTUE	DEFINITION	BIBLE VERSES	DISPOSITION
Live Pure	Chastity	Moral purity and self-control, particularly in the context of sexuality.	1 Thessalonians 4:3-5, 1 Corinthians 6:18-20, Matthew 5:8	Purity and self-discipline
Live Pure	Integrity	Closely tied to honesty, biblical righteousness, and moral character.	Proverbs 11:3, Titus 2:7–8, 2 Corinthians 8:21	Honesty and steadfastness
Speak True	Speaking True	Communicating honestly, accurately, and in alignment with God's principles and standards.	Ephesians 4:25, Proverbs 12:19, Colossians 3:9	Sincerity and clarity
Right Wrong	Justice	Upholding fairness, righteousness, and moral rightness in all aspects of life.	Micah 6:8, Isaiah 1:17, Proverbs 21:3	Fairness and impartiality

HONOR CODE CATEGORY	VIRTUE	DEFINITION	BIBLE VERSES	DISPOSITION
Right Wrong	Kindness	A compassionate and benevolent attitude toward others; showing love, generosity, and consideration without expecting anything in return.	Ephesians 4:32, Galatians 5:22, Proverbs 11:17	Compassion and generosity
Right Wrong	Forgiveness	Letting go of grudges and showing mercy to those who have wronged you.	Matthew 6:14-15, Colossians 3:13, Ephesians 4:32	Mercy and graciousness
Right Wrong	Charity	Generosity and giving to those in need, reflecting God's provision and love.	2 Corinthians 9:7, Matthew 6:1–4, Proverbs 19:17	Generosity and selflessness
Follow the King	Faith	Trust and belief in God's promises, even when circumstances are challenging.	Hebrews 11:1, Proverbs 3:5–6, Romans 15:13	Trust and reliance on God

HONOR CODE CATEGORIES, VIRTUES, AND DISPOSITIONS

HONOR CODE CATEGORY	VIRTUE	DEFINITION	BIBLE VERSES	DISPOSITION
Follow the King	Hope	Confident expectation in God's goodness and the fulfillment of His promises.	Romans 5:5, Lamentations 3:21–23, 1 Peter 1:3–4	Optimism and confidence
Follow the King	Humility	Recognizing one's dependence on God and treating others with respect and honor.	Philippians 2:3-4, James 4:6, Proverbs 22:4	Modesty and respectfulness
Follow the King	Love	Selfless, unconditional, and sacrificial love; the essence of God's nature.	1 Corinthians 13:4–7, John 15:12–13, 1 John 4:7–8	Selflessness and affection
Follow the King	Meekness	A quality stemming from trust in God's sovereignty and a willingness to surrender personal desires.	Matthew 5:5, Galatians 5:22–23, Psalm 37:11	Gentleness and acceptance

HONOR CODE CATEGORY	VIRTUE	DEFINITION	BIBLE VERSES	DISPOSITION
Follow the King	Obedience	Following God's commandments and living in alignment with His will.	John 14:15, Deuteronomy 11:1, Romans 6:17	Willingness and submission
Follow the King	Gratitude	Recognizing and appreciating God's blessings and the kindness of others with a thankful heart.	1 Thessalonians 5:18, Colossians 3:15–17, Psalm 136:1	Heart of thankfulness and appreciation
Shepherd Well	Shepherding	Taking on the responsibilities of caring, guiding, and protecting a community or flock.	John 10:11, 1 Peter 5:2–4, Psalm 23	Care and responsibility

IRON ACADEMY:

PIONEERING DEEP THINKING EDUCATION *for* OVER *a* DECADE

At Iron Academy, we don't follow educational trends—we forge new paths through the wilderness. Over thirteen years ago, as the world rushed headlong into shallow, screen-based learning, we built our Targeted Learning model on the solid rock of biblical wisdom. Like the prudent man who built his house upon the rock (Matthew 7:24–25), we established a foundation that ensures young men master knowledge, develop deep thinking skills, and apply God-given wisdom in real-world battles.

The new book from top global educational researchers, *Developing Curriculum for Deep Thinking,* now affirms what Scripture has always taught: true wisdom requires both knowledge and understanding. As Proverbs 9:10 declares, *"The fear of the Lord is the beginning of wisdom, and knowledge of the Holy One is understanding."* While the world has wandered in the desert of educational experimentation, Iron Academy has been equipping young warriors with minds sharpened to cut through cultural deception. Our Targeted Learning approach recognizes that deep thinking thrives on a structured, knowledge-rich foundation, progressively strengthening intellectual capacity as teachers shepherd students through four levels of mental engagement.

THE DIFFERENCE: A SYSTEMATIC PROGRESSION TOWARD DEEP THINKING

Unlike progressive models that emphasize generic skills without deep knowledge, Montessori methods that rely on self-guided exploration, or classical approaches that focus on rote memorization, detached from immediate application, Iron Academy's Targeted Learning model takes a deliberate, structured approach to deep thinking.

Developing Curriculum for Deep Thinking confirms what we've long known and practiced: deep thinking doesn't happen by chance—it must be cultivated with the intentionality a warrior brings to his training. Just as David didn't defeat Goliath with untested skills, our young men cannot overcome the intellectual giants of our age with undisciplined minds. Our method guides students systematically through A-, B-, C-, and D-Level Learning, ensuring they're equipped to think critically, analyze deeply, and stand firm on the intellectual battlefields of our time.

Will we send our sons into the fray with untested weapons and minds left untrained? Or will we prepare them, as the Apostle Paul urged, to *"put on the full armor of God"* (Ephesians 6:11), including the helmet of salvation that protects and sharpens the mind for God's purposes?

THE ARCHERY ANALOGY: TARGETED LEARNING IN ACTION

An archer doesn't hit the bullseye on his first shot. Through disciplined practice, he refines his stance, accuracy, breath control, and release until his arrows consistently strike the center. This mirrors how men of the Bible prepared for their calling—with diligence, practice, and unwavering commitment to excellence.

Consider the sons of Issachar, who *"understood the times and knew what Israel should do"* (1 Chronicles 12:32). These were men who not only possessed knowledge but applied it with wisdom. At Iron Academy, we train young men to become modern sons of Issachar—warriors who interpret their times and respond with godly insight.

Before students can engage in D-Level Learning—the highest level of critical thought—they must build foundational skills through structured practice. This follows the biblical pattern of preparation. Even Jesus *"increased in wisdom and stature"* (Luke 2:52), growing through a process of development. Just as an archer masters the basics before achieving precision, students progress through A-, B-, and C-Level Learning before they can synthesize, innovate, and create at D-Level. There are no shortcuts; this process repeats with every new learning unit, in every class, every year. This structured, scaffolded approach sets Iron Academy apart as a training ground for young minds prepared to stand firm against cultural deception.

IRON ACADEMY'S TARGETED LEARNING PROGRESSION

- **A-Level: Knowledge Building** – Students name, list, and define core concepts, like an archer learning to hold the bow and nock an arrow properly. This echoes Proverbs 4:7: *"The beginning of wisdom is this: Get wisdom. Though it cost all you have, get understanding."*

- **B-Level: Comprehension & Application** – Students organize, summarize, and apply knowledge, refining skills as an archer learns to draw and release with control. This reflects James 1:22: *"Be doers of the word, and not hearers only."*

- **C-Level: Analysis & Interpretation** – Students critique, compare, and recognize patterns, much like an archer adjusting for wind and distance to perfect their aim. This parallels the Bereans, who *"examined the Scriptures every day to see if what Paul said was true"* (Acts 17:11).

- **D-Level: Synthesis, Innovation & Leadership** – Students craft arguments, solve problems, and create meaningful contributions—the equivalent of an archer striking the bullseye with precision and confidence. This fulfills 1 Peter 3:15: *"Be prepared to give an answer to everyone who asks you to give the reason for the hope that you have."*

BEYOND PASSIVE LEARNING: CULTIVATING TRUE MASTERY

For young men, D-Level Learning is the most engaging and fulfilling experience—and it's equally rewarding for teachers. It transforms education from passive consumption into active creation, much like David, moving from tending sheep to leading a nation with wisdom and courage.

Teachers thrive when they can engage students in meaningful discussions and intellectual debates at the highest levels. Yet modern screen-dependent education remains stuck at A- and B-Level Learning— relying on memorization, multiple-choice assessments, and surface-level engagement. This leaves students disengaged and unprepared for real-world challenges, never hitting the true targets of a great education.

Have we not been warned that *the wisdom of this world is foolishness in God's sight"* (1 Corinthians 3:19)? Will we continue to accept educational approaches that leave our young men spiritually and intellectually unarmed for the battles they must face?

IRON ACADEMY: WHERE EVERYONE WINS

At Iron Academy, teachers begin with the target in mind—D-Level Learning. With this goal set, they methodically guide students through cognitive development stages, ensuring consistent engagement in the highest levels of critical thinking, problem-solving, and leadership.

Unlike conventional models, Iron Academy moves beyond passive learning, transforming students into creators—not just consumers—of knowledge. They form and defend arguments, design innovative solutions, and develop leadership skills that extend far beyond the classroom.

This approach fosters resilience, purpose, and deep thinking—skills surpassing anything offered by screen-dependent, passive environments. Like the faithful servants who multiplied their talents rather than burying them (Matthew 25:14–30), our students invest their God-given intellectual abilities for maximum impact.

Just as an archer finds deep satisfaction in mastering precision, our students experience the fulfillment of mastering their minds, engaging at the highest levels of thought, and preparing for the divine purpose God created them for. They graduate not merely as educated young men, but as warriors equipped for the intellectual and spiritual battles of our time, ready to advance the Kingdom with minds as sharp as their convictions are deep.

"For God has not given us a spirit of fear, but of power and of love and of a sound mind" (2 Timothy 1:7). At Iron Academy, this sound mind is forged through intentional, rigorous educational practices that prepare young men to stand firm in their faith, lead with wisdom, and transform their world for Christ.

THE FIGHT CLUB CURRICULUM SERIES

FIGHT CLUB: A DISCIPLESHIP JOURNEY TO FORGE GODLY MEN

The Fight Club curriculum series offers structured, intensive discipleship programs designed to forge men of conviction, character, and courage. Each workbook in the series includes 12-15 weeks of biblical exploration, personal challenges, and small-group accountability, forming a spiritual training ground where participants are equipped to reject passivity, embrace responsibility, and live with intentionality and strength. A parallel series is also being developed for high school young men— tailored to their unique developmental stage and designed to train them in the same foundational habits of Scripture, brotherhood, and biblical manhood. This program is based entirely on Scriptural imperatives and rooted in the Word of God. It also draws from newly revealed cognitive science and relational discipleship practices that enable true spiritual formation. As J.C. Ryle put it, "He that would understand the true nature of true holiness must know that the Christian is 'a man of war.' If we would be holy we must fight." This conviction lies at the heart of everything Fight Club teaches and trains: holiness is not stumbled into— it is fought for.

This battle for holiness is not waged by willpower alone; it must be undergirded by systems and practices that align with how God has designed the human brain and spirit to grow. The Fight Club curriculum uniquely integrates Scripture with research-proven methodologies—drawing from neuroscience, attachment theory, and relational discipleship—so that true transformation becomes possible, measurable, and lasting. Specifically, it draws from Iron Academy's Targeted Learning model, insights from cutting-edge brain research, and a neuro-relational framework that recognizes how relational connection, emotional regulation, joy, and genuine community form the foundation of deep character and spiritual transformation. Together with the best techniques of spiritual formation and biblical worldview development, this curriculum represents a unique synthesis never before systematized at this depth for men's discipleship and formation.

If you've ever wondered why traditional Bible studies often do not lead to marked spiritual formation, you were right to do so. We have wandered far from the biblical prescriptions for transformation that utilize the entire brain. This curriculum conforms to God's design for learning AND transformation.

For pastors, this is a tool utilizing time-tested and research-proven methods—many of which have never before been systematically applied in Bible studies—to disciple and mobilize men in your congregation. It is built for scale, simplicity, and measurable impact. Men will develop a habit of reading the Bible, understanding the Bible, memorizing the Bible, and applying the Bible to their lives. As a result, they become stronger spiritual contributors within the life of the church—men who can lead, serve, and disciple others with clarity, humility, and biblical conviction. For men, it is a powerful way to finally engage in a Bible study that produces real, lasting growth with brothers who will walk with you. Whether you're starting a group at your church or rallying a few friends, Fight Club will give you everything you need to build biblical manhood in community—helping you grow as a follower of Jesus, become a better man, love your wife well, lead your children with grace, become the spiritual leader of your home you were designed by the Creator of the Universe to be, and shepherd your community with wisdom and conviction.

Each Fight Club curriculum includes a Leader Guide, Participant Workbook, and optional supplemental resources designed to facilitate meaningful conversation, Scripture-based accountability, and applied spiritual growth. These tools can be implemented in churches, community groups, schools, or family discipleship settings. A parallel series for high school young men is also available—equipping churches and families to disciple the next generation of men using the same transformative approach.

Just as Nehemiah rallied God's people to "fight for your brothers, your sons, your daughters, your wives, and your homes" (Nehemiah 4:14), the Fight Club curriculum equips believers to answer that same call today—with biblical clarity, relational strength, and Kingdom purpose.

Fight Club is twelve distinct Bible campaigns to forge godly men. Each 12-15-week campaign anchors men in Scripture while forging character, leadership, perseverance, and legacy. The journey begins with John, forming identity in Christ, and progresses through key biblical texts that challenge men to live boldly, lead sacrificially, endure trials, and build lives rooted in gospel conviction. From the courage of Acts and the commissioning authority in Matthew, to the resilience shaped by James, Peter, and Corinthians, these campaigns cultivate wisdom and spiritual grit.

The series also equips men with doctrinal clarity (Romans, Hebrews), servant leadership (Luke), and vision for lasting legacy (Genesis). Through each book, men grow in relational discipleship, doctrinal depth, and practical holiness—becoming gospel-rooted men who lead their homes, churches, and communities with integrity, humility, and purpose.

For more information on bringing Fight Club to your church or community, or to order materials for your family or friends, visit ironacademy.org/fightclub.

DONATING TO IRON ACADEMY IS AN INVESTMENT IN THE NEXT GENERATION OF CHRISTIAN MEN WHO ARE BEING INTENTIONALLY SHAPED INTO COURAGEOUS LEADERS OF CHARACTER, WISDOM, AND INTEGRITY.

YOUR SUPPORT DIRECTLY EMPOWERS A RIGOROUS ACADEMIC PROGRAM ROOTED IN BIBLICAL TRUTH, MENTORSHIP, AND PERSONAL ACCOUNTABILITY—EQUIPPING YOUNG MEN TO IMPACT THEIR COMMUNITIES FOR CHRIST.

EVERY GIFT HELPS PROVIDE SCHOLARSHIPS, ENHANCE FACILITIES, AND EXPAND OPPORTUNITIES FOR DISCIPLESHIP, ENSURING THAT NO MISSION-DRIVEN STUDENT IS TURNED AWAY DUE TO FINANCIAL BARRIERS.

BY PARTNERING WITH IRON ACADEMY, DONORS BECOME PART OF A TRANSFORMATIVE LEGACY THAT STRENGTHENS FAMILIES, CHURCHES, AND SOCIETY THROUGH GODLY LEADERSHIP.

PLEASE SCAN THE QR CODE OR GO TO:

https://www.ironacademy.org/support/

5f1df3f8-17ca-4d75-9819-7f50eed26bbfR01